Another Look At Life

By

Maureen Wingham

First published in Great Britain in 2019 by Maureen Wingham

Copyright © 2019 Maureen Wingham, all rights reserved.

No part of this publication may be reproduced, stored in retrieval system or transmitted in any form or by any means, electronic, mechanical, photocopying, recording or otherwise without the prior permission of the author.

The moral rights of the author, Maureen Wingham have been asserted.

Written by Maureen Wingham.

CHAPTER ONE

It was a few days after I returned home from hospital where I had reluctantly parted with my gallbladder – albeit by keyhole surgery.

My son was just about to visit me. However some years before he had sustained a spinal injury and subsequent surgery failed to right the problem so by now he was wheelchair bound. Under these circumstances he was unable to access my house in the wheelchair.

However, as I had so recently had surgery he wanted to come and see me so with the help of his wife and a manual wheelchair to say nothing of considerable effort on his part he was visiting me.

Just as my daughter-in-law was overseeing the somewhat tricky, to say nothing of potentially dangerous manoeuvre, my mobile rang. I did not recognize the voice but the man asked for me by name. There was considerable background noise and so frequently one receives sales calls. However, before I dismissed the call the man said 'Chingford' and repeated his name. Well, that was a blast from the past.

The call was from my one-time business partner but he was also godfather to my son and we had not been in touch for some 40 years.

I asked him if he remembered that he had a godson which he did as well as his name. I told him of the coincidence that my son was just coming into my house and also briefly of his present condition.

We chatted for a short while and he said he would phone me again.

By now my son was safely in the house and I told him about the call. He had a number of questions as to why David had phoned after all this time and if he would phone again. Unfortunately my choice of godparents had not been very successful. At the end of the 60s David had become my business partner but I had had to remove him from the business when my son was very young and his godmother had gone to the US in the 80s and remarried.

Over the next few days David called me a couple of times and we spoke about mutual friends and some of the activities he had engaged in during the intervening years. The end of the following month I planned to go into London and I phoned David to see if he wished to meet. I would have about an hour to spare – in the past his timekeeping had been very lax so I was not sure if we would actually manage the meeting. However, when I arrived at the café he was already there. We chatted about some of the past events, I told him about some of the friends we had known long before we were in business who sadly were no longer with us.

I discovered he had finally married his very long time girlfriend whom he had met after his divorce many decades ago. He concluded that to catch up some 40 years we would have to speak again.

I learned that he located me by finding a previous book I had written and then Googled me and came across various references including a Press Release which listed my mobile number.

I told him that one friend – whom he had known from a very early age – often asked me if I had heard from David and I had always given a negative reply.

We had met when we both attended ballroom dancing classes before he had to do his National Service. He was a good-looking young man, tall and dark and a very good dancer. We found that we had many friends in common and we went out together enjoying dancing and the theatre. He was interested in the arts and I was still involved in drama.

As the time went by I used to have parties for my birthday and at Christmas. In those days my parents were prepared to go to the theatre for the evening and the parties went with a swing. However, everyone respected the house and I don't think we even had a broken glass. My mother was quite suspicious when she was stopped in the street by one of my friends asking when I was having another party.

However, there was a jazz club a short distance from the town and apparently David and some friends had asked the band if they would play at a party. I only found out when I looked out of the window just as the party was due to begin. I saw seven guys walking down the middle of the road complete with their instruments. I could see the net curtains down the road twitching and expected that would continue during the evening. On this occasion my parents had agreed to stay out overnight. The party went with a swing. Late in the evening someone drew my attention to the strange noise from the telephone. I discovered that the receiver had been knocked off – in those days the operator could blast a sound down a phone under these circumstances. I replaced the receiver and immediately the phone rang. It was my mother asking if everything was alright. I assured her that it was – although by now I realized there were quite a few people I didn't know – and she told me that if she had not got a reply on that occasion they would have come straight home. After that I looked around and decided we had uninvited guests so I spoke to several of the rugby playing guys and asked them to go round and remove anyone we didn't know. They managed that very successfully.

I remember one evening when David was visiting and we were listening to the news which was announcing the events unfolding with the Hungarian Revolution or Hungarian Uprising. We were both shocked by the news and we discussed the possibility of a fundraising event. We discussed this with other friends and we organized a dance, booked a band and sold the tickets which raised funds that went to a larger organization to assist the people.

One year we went on holiday together to Spain. As I recall we flew to Paris and then went by train down to Spain and stayed in Estartit, a small fishing village, which had one small modern hotel. We made friends with some other English people. The beach was almost deserted and very quiet. One evening we had booked to go to a flamenco show. The dancer was La Chunga who was well-known. Flamenco shows generally have a late start but we found the singers and guitarists playing dominoes in the bar long after the official start time. Eventually the performance was announced. It was well worth the wait, she was a brilliant dancer. I had been learning flamenco dance and was really keen to watch her footwork and all the moves.

I had never particularly enjoyed eating meat because I found it very uninteresting, bearing in mind my early childhood was during WW2 and thus rationing which continued after the war finished. Also my mother cooked the meat until it was well-done, as many people did at that time. During the holiday I discovered steak cooked rare - it changed my whole attitude to red meat. When I returned home I cooked the meat myself and continued to eat rare steaks and roasts for many years. Events in later life would mean a change of diet.

Years later driving through Spain with my first husband we drove past Estartit and it was unrecognizable; there were so many high rise apartment blocks and hotels. It seemed impossible that such a tiny quiet little village could have expanded so much and lose the very Spanish character of the past.

At this time David had worked for a bank although I don't think he was particularly keen on it as he always wanted something more bohemian.

As a child I had taken ballet and tap dance classes. In my teens I found a flamenco dance teacher in London. She had recently arrived from Argentina and ran classes at the rehearsal rooms in Gt. Newport Street in London. I loved flamenco dance and music. Margot had run a dance school in Argentina and she was a very good teacher who ultimately became a friend.

On one occasion Margot was due to dance at a Spanish social event, however at the last minute she could not go and called me and asked me to stand in for her. The only problem was that I was no way fluent in Spanish and they were expecting a Spanish native. So she suggested I fained laryngitis and conducted any conversation via the guitarist!

CHAPTER TWO

Although drama was my first choice one had to earn a living and after a short while as a secretary at a major city insurance company I moved to a temp agency and found myself in the advertising department of a group of five companies. At first I was working on a temporary basis and able to have the odd day off to do a photo-shoot or TV extra work. That which is not revealed to the customer flicking through a catalogue – the corset photographed is too big for the model so there was a huge roll of cotton wool down the back and various pins.

I had auditioned at the Palmers Green repertory theatre and although they did not have a vacancy at the time, whilst I was working in the advertising department the theatre phoned me as they had an ASM vacancy. Unfortunately, the salary was so small that I just could not afford to accept. In retrospect I wondered how different life would have been had I accepted. Prior to that I had auditioned at RADA but as I could not obtain a scholarship my mother would not allow me to ask my father to pay my fees. Another "what if?

However, I found the overall work in advertising interesting as the department covered exhibitions, press advertising, preparing print for brochures, posters and checking response to the advertisements and ensuring these were sent to the correct sales areas. There was always a heavy volume of work and most of it urgent.

By now I had less contact with David although our paths crossed from time to time because I still lived at my parents' house and we had mutual friends and parties.

During my time working in this department I developed my dislike of Management Consultants. I had my appendix removed and was back at my desk sooner than my doctor would have liked. At this time I was the only person working directly with Richard, the Advertising Manager. My office had three desks each of which was piled with papers. The Managing Director had recently been on a visit to the US and returned to appoint Management Consultants. Absolutely snowed under with work these annoying males frequently came into my office with *"are you busy?"* Well, yes it should have been very obvious. Finally I picked up a copy of a large tome and threw it at the door. I was pleased they did not bother me again.

At Richard's suggestion I had decided to embark on advertising studies and enrolled at St. Martin's College in Charing Cross Road, London. He travelled a lot and would request me to meet him at different locations in order to approve print proofs and other work so I could return to the office and proceed with the work. Richard was some seventeen years my senior, he had a good knowledge of food and wine. He had served in WW2 and I understood spent much time in Italy and had certainly appreciated the food and wine – and probably the women. Over time, travel, dinners and working late when he often drove me home, we gradually became involved although I would not have set out to have an affair with a married man. However, I was well aware that he had other affairs. Gradually it progressed to a more serious level although by now he had moved to another company and eventually he said he planned to leave his wife.

We looked at several flats and finally agreed on one in

Holland Park. We started to move in, I had still not told my mother what I was going to do although she already knew I was going out with him and she totally disapproved and we had many arguments. However, shortly after we had the keys to the flat and started to move in, I received a letter from him to say he had changed his mind and could not leave his wife. As I had seen him the day before, this was a massive shock. I could not speak with my mother about it and I got out of the house as soon as possible to go to work.

Once in London I phoned the estate agent to find that Richard had returned the lease unsigned. I went to the flat to discover that he had cleared out all the things that had been taken there. I phoned a girlfriend Margot and arranged to meet her later to talk about what had happened. For days I tried to phone him and could not reach him at his office. I wanted to see him face-to-face. This had been a huge shock to me; he had broken off the relationship by letter and at first would not speak to me to discuss his change of decision.

Later we met on and off and this continued for quite some time afterwards. During this period I travelled with him one weekend on a promotion trip and en route back to London there was a car accident in which I came off worse. The car rolled and I was thrown from the front seat landing on the rear seats and dislocated my elbow and fractured the head of the radius of my right arm. He took me to hospital in the Midlands and after they set the dislocation and X-rayed me, he then had to take me back to London by train and all the way to my parents' home. He would have liked to have put me in a taxi and send me home rather than face my parents. When I got home around midnight I went to bed but insisted on removing my make-up and promptly fainted.

My doctor visited me and arranged for the surgeon to see

me at home after receiving the X-rays from the hospital. About a week later I went into hospital for the operation to remove the piece of bone from my arm. My mother had been both shocked and furious that I had an affair with a married man and we had had numerous arguments on the subject. By the time I was in the accident I then felt that it was probably retribution and terrified that I would die under the anaesthetic and finally I had to discuss it with my father. Once I recovered from surgery there followed months of physiotherapy to get the arm to move properly and be able to turn my hand round in a normal way. When I returned to work my physiotherapy was transferred to the Middlesex Hospital in central London so that I could attend in my lunch hour. I found that hand and arm movements from flamenco dance plus the castanets proved very useful to improve the movement of the fingers.

At this time I was P R Manager for Strelitz fashion and Steegan menswear. I had been appointed to raise the profile of the Strelitz collections, hitherto these had been very classic styles in Irish linen - the company was part of the Stevenson Moygashel fabric company based in Dungannon. However, with the explosion of new and innovative fashion that burst on the scene in the early sixties the company wanted to change their image so the designer produced a range, mostly designed in Irish tweeds mixed with silk and linens, with many Chanel style suits and dress and jacket ensembles. They had developed an excellent colour range and we had been fortunate that the press liked the clothes and we obtained good coverage in the major fashion magazines and newspapers including a colour cover on Flair - a major fashion magazine in the sixties.

CHAPTER THREE

My girlfriend Rosemary who was a journalist also did some holiday tour guide work in Italy and she had an Italian boyfriend who owned a small hotel in the La Spezia area. One year she suggested that I go down there for a holiday. I booked a flight to Paris and then went by train to La Spezia. Someone who escorted me onto the train suggested that I put the large suitcase in the registered baggage compartment. My Italian language was virtually non-existent but as we did at that time I had the necessary phrase book with me. I disembarked at the station only to find that my suitcase had not been off-loaded. I remember charging down the platform, phrase book in hand to no avail. Not a good start to the holiday. When I arrived at the hotel I told Rosemary and she got the hotel staff to start to locate my luggage. In the event it took about a week for it to turn up so by the time I got the case it was nearly time for the return journey. Needless to say I never allowed my luggage to be stowed in the registered compartment again.

In my early twenties I decided that I had to move into a flat in central London. Although my journey home was about an hour from central London the train service was very unreliable and could be difficult to be sure one could catch a train after a theatre visit.

My girlfriend Marjorie and I planned to share a flat. We looked at several and finally decided upon one in Pimlico. At this time we each had relationships with married men – mine still with Richard - we had agreed that the only men we would invite back would be either of these men. The landlord was a barrister and we found we had to be careful because he retained a key and on occasion tried to enter the flat without ringing the doorbell; so we made sure to keep the chain on the door.

At some point I learned that David had left his job at the bank and gone abroad, I understood he was living in Spain.

In the 60s the Studio Club in Swallow Street was very popular, it was frequented by artists as well as many advertising people and the music was good; it was somewhere I could go on my own but usually there would be people I knew so I often called in after work.

During our flat sharing I had discovered that Marjorie could be incredibly moody. So much so that if she was in a bad mood it brought a complete cloud down over the flat as soon as she came home. When I went on a Press Visit to the Balearic Islands my return journey was badly delayed so that I returned to the flat well after midnight; I discovered that she had gone away for the weekend but had completely cleared out the fridge so that there was nothing to eat or drink. Even in central London in 1963 the shops were not open at that time and I had to wait until later on the Sunday to get some provisions. Fortunately Richard had arranged to take me to lunch.

I went to a party with Paul an actor friend but he disappeared to help the hosts arrange the drinks and suddenly this, tall, slim, dark-haired man turned to me and introduced himself as Michael. He offered to take me home, gave me his phone number and asked me to call him. I declined the offer of a lift home, I was a bit wary of Lambretta scooters, and did not call him - at that time I was not used to phoning men I hardly knew to arrange a date.

Over the ensuing months I saw Paul from time to time. Like many actors he often worked at one of the theatre clubs in St. Martin's Lane. One evening I went to the club for a drink when Paul was working and several other people I knew were there. Someone invited me to go across the road to have dinner and I accepted. As we went down the stairs suddenly there was a commotion behind me and Paul went flying past me down the stairs to attack the fellow and clawed his shirt, he was almost like a tiger. I was absolutely stunned and so was my dinner partner. It took several well-built guys to pull Paul off and calm him down. I was not Paul's girlfriend and was totally unprepared for this display of jealousy.

Sometime after our first meeting Michael called me, he wanted to watch a Shakespearian film on television, I must have been interested because I bought this rather flimsy excuse and agreed to him coming to the flat in Pimlico and we watched the film. My flatmate was annoyed, especially after he playfully slapped her bottom; when we took the flat we were each involved in affairs and the agreement was that we would not bring back to the flat men other than those related to these affairs. However, my affair was petering out although it would continue on a lower key for quite a while and I did not see Richard so frequently, I was not expecting to start a new relationship at that time.

I did not hear from Michael again for some time but, as I would discover over the ensuing years, Michael's timing proved uncanny.

I was head-hunted from Strelitz for a P R Manager

position at a large fashion group and my responsibility was for the house making dresses for what were then termed large ladies. I managed to persuade the designer to introduce some more flattering styles and the fashion editors were helpful in giving editorial. There was a monthly newspaper which circulated to some 60,000 customers and I upgraded this to include all aspects of women's wear from lingerie to swimwear plus cosmetics and also holidays. Unfortunately the offices for administration for several companies in the group were in Camden Town long before it became fashionable and about the only café to get any lunch was a typical transport caff type. Fortunately the showrooms were in the West End so I managed to spend part of my time at the showroom.

The group had a very demanding Managing Director and one day I was summoned to a meeting at the Head Office and found that the Marketing Director was also present. The Managing Director had recently returned from the US and I noticed that there was a bolt of fabric draped over an armchair. Somewhat off-putting was that the fabric displayed a full panel print of the Mona Lisa. It transpired that the Managing Director was planning to use this fabric for dresses for the house catering for large ladies. The idea of being asked to present dresses in this fabric to the fashion press was not to be contemplated. When asked my opinion I gave my frank opinion only to find the Director yelling at his Marketing Director *"make her enthusiastic", "make her enthusiastic"*. Absolutely no chance that anyone was going to change my mind.

During 1964 I was making plans to work freelance. I was planning to work from home so obviously I could not do this sharing the present flat but in any case I did not know how much longer I could cope with the moodiness of my flatmate. I knew that a friend was planning to vacate his flat in Marylebone and I was able to secure the lease. I was in a dilemma about telling my flatmate because I really did not think I could stand weeks of moodiness from her. Therefore, I only gave her a very short notice of my intentions; she was furious that I was moving and from the time I had informed her she maintained the silent treatment.

Richard had offered to help me move out and in the middle of this our phone rang, it was Michael. I gave him my new phone number and address and then completed the move. Marjorie never spoke to me again; a year or so later I remember passing her in Baker Street but she completely ignored me. It was a pity for the friendship to end that way. We had previously taken a holiday together in Gibraltar and Tangier but then I had noticed that when I arrived in a club where she was with a man she really did not want me to stay.

I had difficulty obtaining a refund of the deposit on the flat. On one occasion I mentioned this to a lawyer friend of mine. Sometime later my friend phoned me and invited me round for a drink. When I arrived he gave me an envelope with the cash deposit. Apparently through his legal friends another barrister knew my ex-landlord but evidently there was a gambling debt and my deposit was obtained from the landlord.

Soon after I moved into the new flat, I went to the US on a business trip for the fashion company where I was PR Manager; it was a somewhat stressful trip because the company had run a competition and the prize was a trip to New York, Washington and Philadelphia for the winners. The difficulty was that the winners were members of the public and the store buyer where the prize winner had bought her dress plus the area manager responsible for the store, each of them with their partners; a mixture that does not guarantee harmony. I found I had to act almost as a tour manager getting everyone to the right place at the right time and then fitting in business meetings. However, it was good experience.

One evening in the hotel in New York, I had decided to go to bed early but received a phone call from the hotel's Press Officer inviting me down for a drink. She said she was with a group in the cocktail lounge. So I went down but to my surprise found that I was barred from entry by an officious hotel employee informing me that unaccompanied ladies could not be admitted. I had to request that he contact the Press Officer who then came to the entrance with profuse apologies. I suspect that would not happen nowadays.

CHAPTER FOUR

On my return to London I started to work as a freelance PR consultant. In the early sixties there were many designers opening their own fashion houses or boutiques but of course most were on very tight budgets and had little money for PR or promotions so it was difficult to get a good portfolio of well-paid accounts. When clients were secured one could never be sure that they would pay their bills, on time or for that matter at all.

Some designers such as Ivan Goujon had excellent styles with a really good cut but just under-capitalized. He had several excellent collections but cash flow problems eventually resulted in rescue by an Accountant which caused a lack of the design freedom that had made his clothes so attractive. Ivan had designed paper panties which at that time seemed somewhat unusual but this was obviously the attraction for the Accountant.

I had a number of accounts and spent the next few months handling the PR for my clients and constantly chasing new business. Margot Shakespeare had some very innovative designs and used unusual fabrics, but the budget was so small that the fee was not large and eventually took longer and longer to obtain payment. Another client Deborah Newall was also a good designer with a range of cocktail and evening wear but her budget was so tight that she would not agree to photography;

fortunately she made excellent sketches of the clothes and the fashion editors were prepared to use these.

One of the clients opened a boutique in Kensington where the whole of the collection was made of khaki on the WW2 theme. Amazingly all the fashion editors loved it and we had some good coverage in the national newspapers. But once again this company had relied on private finance and when the turnover did not meet the investor's expectations quickly, the next tranche of investment was not forthcoming so again a new company bit the dust. I did manage to get paid but it meant sitting in the reception of the client's office until someone finally emerged with my cheque.

One evening towards the end of 1964 Michael phoned but again I put him off telling him I would be busy for the next couple of months. Some weeks later he phoned again, apparently a musician friend had a flat opposite mine in Crawford Street and this time I capitulated and invited Michael over. It was a fateful decision - although I did not realize at the time - but it set the seal on the rest of my life.

That evening he stayed but I offered him the sofa, he wasn't pushy he just accepted it. However, during the night I awoke to find him standing beside my bed. I made some protestations but acquiesced. Great line I thought when he said that sometimes people had to be persuaded to do what they wanted to do. He was a good lover. He was gentle but inventive.

Michael was an actor but had started out as a singer in the fifties with a band and then moved on to work as a solo singer with various R & B bands and toured in both the UK and overseas. He also worked on some of Jack Good's *'Oh Boy'* series. Then he went to Stanislavsky Studio drama school and later appeared in *'Fings Ain't Wot They Used T'Be'* at Stratford East and other projects with Joan Littlewood. He appeared in the film *'Some People'*. By the time I knew him he was working on various commercials and other film work. However, what really interested him was song writing.

Michael did not just enter my life he was already living with me. I learned that he had been married but had just been divorced. Sometimes he would talk about it and about the baby they had that was a thalidomide baby and had died at birth. Apparently the marriage had been very stormy and he had married because Margaret fell pregnant. It seemed that he had taken the death of the baby very badly and apparently at that time the hospital policy meant that they would not discuss the death with him or even let him see the baby.

Shortly after Michael moved in I stopped seeing Richard. I noticed the complete contrast as Richard was some seventeen years my senior and very cynical but Michael had much more soul, was much more spiritual. He would analyse the way people expressed things and could be very persuasive. Michael was about a year younger than me and in contrast to Richard obviously seemed very young but on the other hand had way more street experience than me.

In many ways it was a strange relationship. I was working and although I worked from home had to be up and about for an office-hours start. Clients were wont to phone early, especially if The Times had misspelt their name or left out the stockist list! Whereas Michael would surface around lunch-time take the afternoon getting ready and then go out in the evening. I never went with him, he went to parties, met up with other musicians, went to clubs. I never really knew where Michael was when he was out, unless, of course he was working. Some evenings he would stay home.

Shortly after he started living with me, I went away

on business and on my return he was not at the flat. It was then I realized how important he had become. I thought he had left but eventually he came home in the early hours. This became a pattern. He would return in the early hours and then often make himself a meal and come to bed. When I got up in the morning I would find I had to clear up the kitchen which really annoyed me. Although, he would often promise to be more helpful it seldom worked.

Because he had spent many years on the road with bands his whole lifestyle was geared to late nights and not rising until late morning or lunch time. Then would come the times when he stayed out all night.

I had already discovered that he could go out for a packet of cigarettes and come back ten days later. One Sunday I went out to post some letters and as it was a lovely day decided to take a walk in Regents Park. Michael had been out for some time before I went out but when I returned and went into the flat I found Michael's trousers and shirt on the floor outside the bathroom. Apparently he had forgotten to take his keys when he went out and when he returned had managed to get the street level door open but had climbed through the landing window and across the roof to get into the flat via the open bathroom window.

One evening he told me that he smoked marijuana; I was completely innocent about drugs as neither I nor any of my friends used them. Although it was the early sixties, not everyone was as high as a kite. I also discovered that he took 'pep' pills but prescribed by his doctor when he was touring and, of course, it had become a habit and the doctor continued to prescribe. This made it more difficult to keep tabs on what was going on and of course how he could stay up all night. I had never experimented with drugs and had no intention of doing so but Michael never made any attempt to persuade me to the point that if there were musicians around that were smoking he made very sure that no-one offered anything to me; he was very protective.

Many days he would work on his music but he had met up with Pat, a hairdresser who worked at a West End men's salon. Michael was most impressed because Pat had already earned royalties on compositions but Pat mostly provided the music whereas Michael's strong suit was lyrics.

There were many late nights because once Michael returned home and started to play songs to me I would stay up as long as possible to listen often getting very little sleep before I had to be up again for work. One of the songs he was writing was *'Thirty Years'* based on the great train robbery. Michael was fanatical about editing and re-editing and re- re-editing songs and therefore did not finally publish at the time.

However, Pat's influence on him became quite marked. He would stay out more and more, often telling me that he had been at Pat's flat. Pat played piano and I always felt that he encouraged Michael to stay.

The absences upset me and often really annoyed me and there were times when he disappeared for several days. Several times I decided the relationship was not going anywhere and I would start to pack up his things ready to throw him out, but when he did return somehow I never went through with it. In many ways he was very honest saying that he could not make any promises that he could change his ways.

Frequently, I tried to persuade him that Pat was not a good influence but Michael was very impressed by money and he really thought that working with him could help with successful song writing.

I learned that Michael had performed *'Call Me'* in a film entitled *'London in the Raw'*. I assumed this was an adult film but wanted to hear him singing - I heard all the song-writing and singing he did at home but had never heard a real performance. I discovered the film was playing at a cinema in the West End and there was a late evening performance. Michael was out and I decided to take myself down to the cinema only to find a line of men in raincoats buying tickets. A bit off-putting, but I was determined not to back out. However, as I went to buy my ticket the Manager appeared and asked if I was aware of the type of film it was. I put my PR hat on and said that one of my clients was singing the title song and I wished to hear it. He did not let me buy a ticket, just took me up to the circle and found me a seat away from the other patrons. The manager walked around periodically to see everything was alright. I stayed a while and was able to hear the song and several reprises then left and took a taxi home. Some days later I told Michael I had been to see the film he appeared shocked that I had seen the film which explored the sex scene in London in 1964. Ironically, this film has recently been digitised and released on DVD with only a '15' rating.

CHAPTER FIVE

One weekend I went down to see my parents. On the Saturday morning I phoned to speak with Michael but a girl answered the phone. Extreme sense of humour failure on my part but she said that Michael had just gone to the shops. I was seething and promptly collected my things and took the next train into London. By the time I reached the flat of course Michael was there, everything in order and no sign of other visitors. He said that his friend had been there and the girl was the friend's girlfriend. I wanted to believe it but was not convinced. I asked him where he thought the relationship was heading and he said until death us do part.

Michael came back around breakfast time one morning with a fellow he introduced as Mitch, a roadie. They had something to eat and then Mitch left. I did not like the man very much and did not really trust him. Michael did not seem to know him well; it seemed to be a casual acquaintance

The flat had an entry system which allowed you to open the street level front door from the flat but there was no way to find out who it was. However, some days later there was a knock on the door of the flat, when I opened it Mitch was standing on the landing. I told him Michael was out but he asked to wash his hands saying he had had some problems with his car, he then left. Michael was not too pleased he had just called unannounced. About a week later, we were preparing to go to a party being held for Election Night by a friend of mine. We were getting ready and I was in a robe about to dress, when the bell rang and Mitch arrived. Michael spoke with him but said that we were going out so Mitch offered us a lift across to Bloomsbury.

Halfway through the party, Michael started to get very edgy and wanted to go home. So we left the party and took a taxi home. When we got there and opened the door, it was to find that the flat had been burgled. The television, Revox tape recorder, my suede coat and Grundig tape recorder had gone and it seemed a set of keys had gone. I was very distressed by this invasion of my home and went to call the police. However, Michael was sure the culprit was Mitch and thought that he could find him and retrieve the goods. He called his friend Gordon who lived opposite and the two of them went out. Gordon's girlfriend kept me company for a while but I was very worried about the missing keys, everything seemed so unsafe alone in the flat.

The next day I called the police and they visited and took notes. Then I was able to call the insurance company. Over the next few weeks Michael spent a lot of time out especially over-night and I did not sleep, eventually I found him and he came back so I could get a night's sleep.

He told me that one night he had found Mitch and called a passing policeman but Mitch talked his way out and the police did not follow through.

I was still really annoyed about the burglary; I had very black and white views about such things and believed that the culprit should be found and dealt with.

Some weeks later when Michael had once again not

come home I went over to Finchley to a studio I knew he used; I was walking down the road when suddenly I spotted Mitch with another fellow. I decided to follow them and followed them all the way to a flat in a nearby road. I went back to the underground station and phoned the police at Paddington Green. They sent a car to collect me so that I could show them the flat. When we got there they went to the flat but came back and asked me to go with them to identify Mitch. So that meant I had to go into the flat with the police. Apparently the other man in the flat was already known to the police. Of course, our belongings were not there but the police took me from room to room to look at television sets and other equipment. Then they told Mitch he had to go to the station with them. However, they did not request another car so this meant that I had to travel in the same car with Mitch sitting in the back with two officers.

I was at Paddington Green for some time. A detective kept going to question Mitch and then returned to ask me more details. Finally, he came back and said that he was certain Mitch had been the person who committed the burglary but that they could not prove it. The detective suggested that maybe my boyfriend might like to 'teach him a lesson'. I asked what happened in that case should Mitch fall and hit his head. The detective did not have any answer to this.

A few days later Michael came home and I told him what had happened. He seemed rather concerned about my actions.

CHAPTER SIX

I learned that the Vicar at the Parish Church at home was holding Confessions one Friday evening (not a regular occurrence in C of E churches). I always had a guilt trip about the affair I had had and also that I was living with someone but not married. I decided to go to the Confession. However, I was totally unprepared for the outcome. Without confessionals in the church, the vicar seated himself on a raised dais over in a side chapel. At the appropriate time each person went to kneel at the dais and make the confession. I confessed to living with my boyfriend but that we weren't married. Before I could finish the vicar instructed me to return to my seat and stay there until after the service and he would speak with me. I had expected some form of penance and reprimand but now did not know what to expect. After the rest of the congregation had departed the vicar came back to speak with me. I explained that my boyfriend had only recently been divorced and that he was not looking to marry again so soon. The vicar told me that I must regularise the situation - either marry or cease the relationship - by the next time I came to the church or I would be excommunicated.

I was absolutely shattered. I went to my parents' house but they were out returning about an hour later. By this time I had helped myself to some of my father's Scotch but was still shaking. When I explained the encounter to my father he was really annoyed. Although he was strict he thought the vicar had over-reacted at this time. I did not tell Michael about this encounter because I thought he may view it as pressure to marry.

Life went on as normal, me looking after various fashion clients, arranging to show their collections and Michael either writing or out and about. One day one of my clients had a Press Show in the morning and, of course, Michael had not returned the previous night but I knew he had an audition that day; his agent had asked me to make sure he got to the audition on time. I had already phoned round everywhere I could think of and left messages but I had to leave to get to the client's showroom.

When I returned mid-afternoon, I walked into the flat to find various clothing strewn round the living room as well as corks from champagne bottles and thence into the bedroom where Michael was asleep. I could not wake him. I was absolutely furious as he had obviously missed the audition. Eventually, I managed to wake him to find that when he had come in he had taken sleeping pills. Of course, he had totally forgotten the audition. Many years later I learned that he had been to some very wild party - he couldn't remember where - all he seemed to remember was something about Battersea Power Station.

One evening he was getting ready to go out and meet Pat. Not surprisingly he had not returned by the time I went to bed. However around 6am the next morning I awoke with a start with the feeling that there was something very wrong. I had appointments most of the day so had to go out but when I returned at the end of the afternoon there was no sign of Michael or that he had returned to the flat so, I then phoned Pat. The phone was answered by a man whose voice I did not recognise and I asked if Michael was there. I was told that if he was a friend of Pat I should go and buy the Evening News as this might tell me where my friend was. I grabbed a coat and ran down to Baker Street to get the paper. When I returned I scanned it for information. Finally, I found a small piece saying that Pat and another man called Brian and Gerry Grant had been arrested for a drugs offence.

Now I knew the name Dean was the name he used for acting although his real name was Michael Eaton but he often introduced himself to people as Dean. I recollected that one or two musicians who had phoned for him had referred to him as Gerry but I could not be sure that the person referred to in the paper was, in fact, Michael. I did not know what to do. I had no idea how to deal with this type of situation I had no experience or even experience via any friends. I did not know anyone who had been arrested. At this time I still did not know if it was Michael involved in whatever had taken place.

I carried on for some days and eventually it was over a week before I received a phone call from a girl who announced herself as the girlfriend of Brian - neither of whom I had known. She told me that Michael was on remand in Brixton and wanted me to visit him. She told me what I had to do to go and visit.

I took the train to Brixton and came out to find the bus that would go past the prison. Very quietly I asked the conductor to let me know when I got to the stop for the prison. Subtlety was obviously not the conductor's forte, when we were approaching the stop he called out, *''ere you are luv this one for Brixton'*. I had already got the headscarf and dark glasses as some form of being incognito. It really was a ghastly place and the formalities one had to go through to actually see the person were quite demeaning. When I saw Michael he did not look well and I tried to find out what had happened.

It transpired that he and Pat were going to a party. Pat was in Brian's car but Michael was travelling in another car with someone he knew as an acquaintance but not a friend. He told me that the cars were stopped in Russell Square and the police ordered everyone out of both cars. When I got home I called Jeffrey, a lawyer friend of mine. I knew he specialised in criminal law and took legal aid cases. Jeffery agreed to take the case and made the arrangements.

The next hearing was about a week later and I went to the Court. So far Michael had not given his address so that he had not compromised my address but Jeffery had managed to supply the address without it being disclosed which protected me especially as I was working from home and clients would not have been impressed.

The bail was set at two sureties of £1000 each - a lot of money at that time. Curiously, Brian who had admitted he owned the drugs, I learned they were found in a suitcase in his car, managed to get the bail immediately. He was an advertising salesman for Tatler magazine and one of the sureties was a director of a Knightsbridge advertising agency. After a couple more hearings Pat had managed to organize bail but I did not have those resources and although Michael gave me a list of people to phone including his agent and various actors that he had worked with no one was too keen to come forth. Mostly they did not want to be associated with anything to do with drugs but also he had a reputation to be somewhat unreliable. Also he would not have his parents informed therefore he could not ask them for assistance.

As the weeks went by Michael had contacted his ex-wife Margaret. She owned her own flat and apparently had some private income. She contacted me but said that she was disinclined to be a surety because she thought that he might run out on her. Finally, Michael was looking very unwell and I was really very concerned about his health. I phoned my mother and said I wanted to speak to my father. When I explained the situation to Daddy he was annoyed he had not been told earlier but he agreed to act as one surety based on his house. When Margaret learned this she agreed because she thought that Michael would not let down my father. So I had to go to the police station in Holborn with my father and then Margaret went there also. The police tried to interview me but as I had no idea what had been going on, they gave up.

At the next hearing the bail for Michael was reduced to two sureties of £500 pounds each. This time Michael came home. For me the advantage was that whilst on bail he had to be at home every night.

Jeffery set up a meeting with Michael but Jeffery told me that he was concerned that Michael was not defending himself properly. Michael seemed very concerned about evidence Pat would give rather more than defending himself. He seemed very concerned about, I suppose with hindsight, dropping other people in trouble or may be reprisals.

I could not understand why Michael would not do everything possible to defend himself because he most certainly was not selling drugs and an entire suitcase of marijuana takes money to buy and anyway Brian had admitted ownership of the drugs.

Michael was certainly getting very worried about the case. He had still not informed his parents that he had been arrested and did not intend to.

The weeks went by and then the police came to give us the date of the trial to be held in December 1965.

My grandmother had died just before that and I learned that the funeral was the same day as the trial started. It was my maternal grandmother and my mother would have preferred me to attend the funeral but my father gave me the go ahead to support Michael at the trial. So Michael and I went to the court. We met the barrister and ran through the case; he said that the Judge hearing the case was really tough on drugs, apparently one of the most hard-line at that time. Not comforting news for either of us. The barrister said that there might be a chance that the court would allow bail overnight but my father would have to be at the court. I phoned my father and he said he could come in to London before the end of the hearing for that day. Margaret had attended the Court with her boyfriend and she decided to phone Michael's father to let him know what was happening. However, by the end of the day the prosecution would not allow bail to be continued for any of them so I went home alone and it had been a fruitless journey for my father.

The next day it seemed really obvious that things were not going well. Apparently the cars in which they had been travelling were stopped in Russell Square and the police instructed everyone to get out of the cars. As Michael was in the first car with an acquaintance he walked back to speak to Pat to ask what was happening. In this time the driver of the car he had been travelling in got back in the car and drove off. With several police cars around it seemed very strange that the police were incapable of stopping or, at least, catching the departing car and apprehending the driver. It seemed that they never managed to find the car or the driver, get the index number and no one seemed to care about it. Some years later we found that one of the detectives handling the case was involved in a corruption matter and subsequently jailed.

The judge even told Michael to *'speak up you're an actor aren't you?'* Whilst Brian had pleaded guilty both Pat and Michael pleaded not guilty. However, the outcome was that they all received the same sentence of three years. This was shattering, I was absolutely devastated and was not able to see Michael or speak to him after the hearing.

I had difficulty to find out where he had been taken and when I eventually found he had been taken to Wormwood Scrubs I had to wait for a visiting permit. It was truly awful but at the same time interesting to watch many visitors chatting to each other and comparing the various jails like other people might compare hotels. Michael decided that he wanted to lodge an Appeal but this was not successful; the Appeal judges concluded that there was no technical legal basis to overturn the sentence. He was informed that he would serve for two years and that the release date was 12 January 1968. A date I hung onto throughout the time.

After a short while he was transferred to an open prison near Bristol. So visiting meant taking the train to Bristol and then a bus out to the country area. I found it very embarrassing having to ask which bus to take and also asking the conductor to let me know the stop at which to alight. On leaving the visit in bad weather it meant standing out in the open on a country lane to wait for the bus. One day when the weather was especially bad the visitors were informed they could remain in the waiting room until it was time for the bus. I stayed in the room reading, I could hear the conversations around me where visitors were complaining about their relatives being in prison. I was hoping no-one would address a question to me because I still maintained that if someone was guilty then they could hardly expect anything else. Eventually one woman spoke directly to me. Even now I was not prepared to agree with their argument I replied accordingly but hoped I did not get lynched. Finally, I decided it might be better to stand in the rain to await the bus than continue to wait inside.

Not long before Christmas I was shopping in D H Evans and I met Adela – a friend I had known when I lived at home – with her mother. I knew that her husband Stan had a serious illness and during the conversation Adela told me he was doing well and expecting to come home from hospital for Christmas. Some nights later I had a vivid dream depicting Stan in a hospital bed with Adela and other relations standing around and that he died. The next morning the image was still so vivid I phoned my mother and asked her to check the local paper for any news. She phoned me to tell me that there was a notice announcing Stan's death. I found this very unnerving. When I told a girlfriend about this she asked me to try to avoid dreaming about her.

Returning from one visit to Michael on the train I met Brian's girlfriend; she told me that she was provided with a first class ticket for her journey and a chauffeured car between the station and prison. She said she would not visit otherwise. I suppose it made sense; her boyfriend admitted owning the drugs and was immediately provided with bail so it really seemed that there was plenty of money from that source. After some time Brian escaped and as far as I know was never heard of again.

This was a very fraught time for the relationship. I was totally in love with Michael but equally utterly disorientated by the situation. I did not know anyone who had been arrested let alone jailed and neither did any of my friends so it was regarded as a very unacceptable situation. The few friends I had taken into my confidence were all keen to tell me to forget the relationship. Of course, I also had to continue with my work and make absolutely sure that no information about this situation filtered through to my clients.

CHAPTER SEVEN

During 1966 I spent my time juggling between servicing the PR accounts, showing the collections to the press; pitching for new business and visiting Michael when permitted. Fortunately at that time I had quite a lot of friends in London and when not working I was able to go out and living in Marylebone gave me easy access to theatres and cinemas as well as London's art galleries. From time to time I also went to the studio to do some flamenco practise.

Michael's ex-wife Margaret presented some problems insofar as she decided to remain in contact with me. I knew from what Michael had told me that she could be a bit of a mischief-maker and I found I was treading a very fine line. Margaret started to phone me and invite me to parties, I was torn between going and the possibility that she would lead Michael to believe that I was being unfaithful and declining the invitation and finding that she told him I had been unpleasant to her. Not a situation I was used to as my girlfriends did not behave in that manner. Furthermore, Margaret did not work and therefore could party all night whereas I had to be up and out to appointments. One night she and her boyfriend rang the doorbell well after midnight inviting me to a party and I had great difficulty in getting them to understand that I could not go but without offending. Years later I learned that my fears had not been unfounded apparently she had told Michael about me going to a party!

In 1966 a friend gave me a kitten, I already still had my other cats but they were at my parents' house. She was very pretty brindle and I named her Honey. As I was living near Baker Street it was not possible to let her out so I used to take her out on a lead for walks close to the flat or even down Baker Street. In many ways she was dog-like when she heard unfamiliar footsteps on the staircase she would growl.

She loved to play retrieve with silver paper balls and would take these to visitors to ask them to play with her. She was inventive with a toilet roll – long before the Andrex puppy – if the bathroom door was open. One day I returned to find she had pulled all the paper into the sitting-room and shredded it. Not content with that she had taken a couple of soft toys from my bedroom and put them on top of the pile and added an item of my underwear. She was also very protective, if someone visited and sat on the sofa she jumped up, walked along the back and down between us. The first time I took her down to my parents I took her on the lead on the underground and the train. It was a quiet time of day and she was very good. However, I bought her a carrier basket for the return journey.

One Bank Holiday weekend I met a girlfriend for lunch and when I returned I noticed that the key plate on the front door seemed loose when I inserted the key. I wondered if it had been tampered with but went into the flat and everything seemed alright. However, the next day I checked it again and it was definitely loose and I called the police. An officer came round and when he looked he said someone had undoubtedly tampered with it and then asked if I had a dog. I said, *"no but I do have a cat who growls at unfamiliar footsteps"* so he said she had probably saved me from being burgled.

An ex-colleague from a PR agency I had worked at telephoned and informed me that another colleague was coming back to England and invited me to dinner. It seemed a perfectly uncontroversial invitation and I accepted. We all went to dinner and afterwards they drove me back to my flat and suggested coffee; so they came up to the flat and I went to make coffee. However, I discovered that one of them had gone to check the car but after a while did not return. Too late I realized that the whole evening had been set up for the visiting colleague and had to evade the groping and get him out of my flat. It was a very tiresome way to end the evening and unexpected as there had never been any relationship with either of them other than purely business. Nowadays I suppose this would come under the '#Me Too' hashtag but in those days we just dealt with it and carried on.

Although this was not the only time I had to avoid groping. At social or business events I met men who invited me to dinner and took me home. As far as I was concerned there was no emotional involvement it appeared to be just friendly until the occasion when the fellow came in for coffee and expected rather more. I found the recently divorced rather tedious as they ended up by complaining about their ex-wife; this was definitely the signal to suggest it was time for them to go home.

The year went by with presentations, fashion shows and pitches for new business. To say nothing of the client who would ring me up late at night to talk about her 'ungrateful' daughter for whom they had just launched a separate fashion label. I hoped I said aha and um in the right places. One weekend the client invited me to tea on the Sunday, they lived in a large apartment block in St. John's Wood and whilst the maid served tea to the client and me her husband stretched out asleep on the sofa. As the year was drawing to a close the client portfolio was looking quite good.

In the week before Christmas I phoned home during the morning and was surprised that there was no reply. Eventually I reached my mother to learn that my father had been taken to hospital having suffered a heart attack. I went down to the hospital that evening to visit and he was quite cheerful. I was able to tell him that work was looking quite hopeful for the following year. The next day my mother told me not to travel down again. A girlfriend was in hospital nearby in Marylebone so I went to visit her as I knew she did not have anyone else to visit.

The following day I wanted to phone the hospital to enquire but intuition kept holding me back and delaying the call. Eventually around 11am.I called the hospital, immediately I knew something was wrong as they got the Sister to speak with me. The Consultant was doing his rounds and had informed my father he could go home for Christmas but before the Consultant had finished the ward round my father had another heart attack. They were working on my father at the time I phoned. They had not had time to phone my mother. So I called my mother and she immediately went to the hospital.

By this time David was working for a media company in London and I phoned to ask if he could drive me to the hospital as I thought it would be quicker than taking the underground and then the train; also I could do with the company and he had known my father. However as I was travelling from central London it took me longer to get there. Christmas traffic did not help but by the time I arrived my father had died. In spite of the previous heart problems he had suffered it was still a shock and tremendous loss. My father had always been so reliable and good with advice and suddenly I was bereft of this stable rock that had been so dependable. I had to go back to London to collect some things and my cat in order to go to mothers for Christmas. I found that journey back home difficult; on the underground it was crowded and there was a group of young men singing *'Silent Night'* which had been a favourite of my father.

It was a very bleak Christmas. My father died on 22 December - the day before my mother's birthday. I had been due to visit Michael on Boxing Day but, of course, had to telephone and ask them to inform him of my father's death and that I could not visit.

The Vicar at the Parish Church kept calling to endeavour to inveigle my mother into having the service at his Church. However, apparently my father had previously told my mother that he wished the service to be held at the chapel at the cemetery. He disliked this Vicar and also had been very upset by the encounter I had previously had with the Vicar. On the evening of Christmas Day, he called again and I answered the doorbell, let him in and showed him to the dining room and promptly fainted. Naturally, my mother was concerned - I am not prone to fainting - and she called an ambulance. All I remember was the Vicar standing around saying that he must get back for choir practise whilst I was put into the ambulance.

The funeral was held after New Year; David and a few other friends attended and then I went back to my flat and tried to throw myself into work. Michael told me later that he had requested compassionate leave to go to the funeral but it was refused.

When I returned to the flat I telephoned someone who had called before Christmas regarding a proposed PR assignment, however, due to my father's death I had called later than the date arranged and the potential client dismissed the matter of my bereavement and decided that I had missed the opportunity.

With Michael away and the death of my father I found it very difficult to sleep and found myself doing housework late at night, once even cleaning the windows after midnight much to the surprise of a passing policeman. Later that year we held a Memorial Service for my father at *St. Brides Church,* Fleet Street London, many of my friends attended.

I was working for clients such as Radley dresses who had a range of mid-priced dresses many of which were well received by the fashion press. Also Felix couture which made excellent coats and all the garments were beautifully finished. By the latter part of the sixties the type of fashion editor was changing – in the early sixties they usually came to the showroom very well dressed but with the changes the Managing Director of Felix took me to one side to ask if the editor in the showroom was really from one of the top broadsheet newspapers because to say she looked scruffy would be an understatement; he could not understand how someone looking that scruffy could appreciate the clothes that Felix made.

At one point I was contacted by an ex-editor of one of the fashion magazines who was at the time assisting some American film people. Apparently they were trying to put together funds for a film project. They wanted some short-term assistance with meetings and secretarial work. I agreed to meet them. It mostly consisted of sitting in meetings and typing a few documents for them. On one occasion they had arranged a meeting with a very well-known author at her house in West London. The fellow who had written the script was with his muse (or mistress). They had booked some actors to attend this meeting to read through some scenes. When one of the actors arrived I immediately connected.

When the meeting finished I went out with the actor and he came back to the flat. Sometime later he stayed at the flat. I think he had just broken up with his girlfriend, also an actress. We were together for several weeks.

CHAPTER EIGHT

Before my father died we had discussed the possibility that my parents would sell their house and we would buy a house together in central London which would then be split into two apartments thus giving me the possibility of a larger apartment. My father had been quite keen on this idea and during the year before his death I had been looking at houses in the Islington area. I found a property which had a N.7 postcode but unfortunately at that time the Halifax Building Society decided that N.7 was not quite 'up and coming'. After his death my mother and I discussed this plan and she said that as my father had agreed to it she would honour his agreement and I should continue to look for another property.

By this time the Canonbury area of Islington already had a substantial swathe of properties renovated so the prices were higher therefore it was necessary to look at the next area which was Barnsbury. I don't think my mother's relatives thought it was a wise choice for her as the family home was close to the forest and she would effectively be moving into an inner city area. They obviously would not have commented if my father had still been alive.

The estate agents responsible for my flat in Crawford Street informed me that it was time for them to undertake an inspection of the flat for the renewal of the lease. I was not supposed to have pets, so I put my cat into her carrier and walked down the road to my girlfriend Marlene who lived in Paddington Street. I took her litter tray as well and left her there for the afternoon. The agents were duly satisfied and the lease was renewed. I then went back to collect Honey and bring her home. When I finally moved my girlfriend Rosemary took over the remainder of the lease.

During 1967 I added house-hunting to my other activities and eventually found a four-storey Victorian property in the Barnsbury area of Islington. It needed renovation, rewiring, central heating, and of course decorating. Eventually I managed to secure a mortgage - not especially easy as a single woman working freelance - but at least in 1967 a letter from the accountant was sufficient to make this application successful. I moved in October 1967 and promptly was surrounded by the builders.

For some reason these builders decided that they had to commence at 7am but by 9am they were sitting on the floor in my kitchen having breakfast. As usual with this type of work there were various problems mostly where the builders tried to persuade me to accept work that was to their satisfaction but not to mine. It was imperative that the work finished before the end of the year because by Christmas my mother would be moving into her apartment in the house. I seemed to spend a lot of time clearing up after the builders. But at last the house was finished.

Whilst Michael was away it was difficult to assess his actual feelings towards me. He wrote to me once a month but only to send a visiting order. He did not at any time ask me to wait for him and sometimes could be quite sulky during my visit. On one occasion he took this to the extent that he did not speak to me for the first part of the visit, and this was one of the few occasions when we were permitted to go out into the grounds and walkabout; I threatened to leave and take the next bus back to the station unless he behaved in a more friendly manner. Another man nearby realized what was happening and reprimanded him; and then he changed his mood and the rest of the visit went on smoothly.

I certainly did not understand this behaviour but then of course I was totally out of my depth in the entire situation. With hindsight I imagine that it was difficult to be incarcerated and then only see someone else for a short period and not know what was going on outside. Although his sentence had been three years he was going to be released after two years and the date for this was the 12 January 1968. I spent the two years with that date firmly fixed in my mind and that was the date to which I was working for the whole time.

In September 1967 my cousin Stuart was getting married; and this had been the first family event that my mother would have to attend since my father's death and although I was not particularly keen to attend this wedding as it meant I would have to change the date for a visit to see Michael I decided to accompany my mother to the wedding. At the wedding I met Robert one of Stuart's friends who offered to drive me back to London at the end of the reception. He seemed pleasant enough and I went out with him a few times. However, as far as I was concerned this was incidental to Michael's return.

Since my father's death my mother had been coming into town a few times a week and helping with administration and phone calls whilst I was out. At that time it wasn't so usual to have parents working in the office (although my lawyer employed both his mother and father) so when I was asked the name of my secretary I said 'Mary' and from that time onwards she was known to all clients and later publishers as Mary.

Before Michael was released in January he would have a week of home leave which he could have taken around September, however, he wanted to leave this until closer to the time of his release so in the event he did not take this leave until November. Of course, by November I had already moved into the house in Islington and was surrounded by builders working all day. Also my mother was coming to the house several days a week to help me with work in the office as she would be moving in soon.

When Michael arrived at the house I was obviously quite excited but I found that he had already made an arrangement to meet with Pat later that afternoon. I went into the West End with him and left him after he had met up with Pat. Although of course he was going to have to ensure that he was at home in the evening I found it very difficult to adjust to the somewhat chaotic lifestyle that I had lived with him before he was arrested. In the interim period apart from the distress I had had a much more organized routine for my life. The following day he told me that he was going to visit his parents, which of course was understandable. When he returned from that visit his friend Pat came to the house and they worked on some songs.

Somehow this meant that the week which I had looked forward to was fast disappearing and I had hardly spent any time with him at all. I asked him where he intended to live when he was released in January and although he told me that it would be with me I suppose my romantic side wanted him to tell me that it was because he loved me, whereas he just said: '*well where else would I go?*' During this week he had also informed me that he did not wish to do any more commercials or acting he wanted to concentrate on song writing. From the very practical financial viewpoint this was somewhat worrying because it meant that he would be unlikely to be earning any income for quite a while and the very real possibility that I would have to subsidize all the living expenses and whatever else he wished to do.

CHAPTER NINE

During 1966 and 1967 in addition to the public relations work that I was doing David, a long-time friend, had persuaded me to start a media representation partnership where we represented foreign media for selling advertising and would specialize in travel media. At first I was not particularly interested in this; I had worked as an advertising manager on the client side and was fully aware that 'space selling' was not very well regarded. However, of course, when dealing with foreign media it meant a slightly different approach had to be taken. During this period David was already working for another representation company and he let me know about any publications which he had come across and I would then make contact with the publishers.

As I had been on my own during 1966 and the early part of 1967 it had not mattered too much that the work I did on the representation partnership was mostly being done in the evenings even so it was very annoying when David arranged to call to discuss the magazines and then arrived towards the end of the evening. I had known David since I was about sixteen and I knew that timekeeping was not his forte nevertheless it was still irritating that he constantly arrived late. By the time I moved to the new house in October 1967 I had to give David an ultimatum: either he left his existing job and worked on the media representation with me on a full-time basis or I dissolve the partnership. Finally he decided to take the plunge and joined me working on media representation on a full-time basis.

The few friends who knew about Michael had all given me advice that I should have nothing more to do with him and of course David added his concerns to this once he was working with me full-time. The office was based in the house and David's main concern was just in case Michael had another problem and it involved the address of the company. Needless to say my mother was not at all happy about me continuing a relationship with Michael; she had been quite pleased when I met Stuart's friend Robert. Robert was a qualified engineer working for a major company and of course worked very regular hours and similarly was paid a regular annual salary.

Although for the past two years I had fixed the date 12 January 1968 in my mind, the date when Michael would be home, after the home visit I gave a lot of thought to the situation and whether I should or should not let Michael live with me again in January 1968 and I decided that it might be better if he got his own flat for a short while. I intended that to mean that we would still see each other and then possibly live together again once he had adjusted to being back in circulation. I was pretty certain that once he was out he would be on the town most evenings or else closeted with Pat and that I would hardly see him thus probably upsetting myself.

Before the home leave I had had to be interviewed by the probation officer and when I made the decision that Michael should not live with me immediately upon release I went back to the probation officer to discuss this as I did not wish that it would in any way adversely affect

Michael. I was told that they would tell him, however, I requested a visit - when he finished the home leave he had said that he did not want another visit until he was released. So when I went down to see him I explained my reasoning and, of course, he said that he understood and that he would come and collect his belongings on the day he came out; it transpired that he had not really listened and had assumed that I meant that I did not wish to continue a relationship with him.

As 12 January grew closer I became more nervous about the decision I had made - it was a practical decision made with my head but certainly not with my heart. When the actual day came and I had his cases packed ready for him my resolve was beginning to wane. I had assumed he would come during the day. David had been in the office all day and my mother was in her flat and it was very difficult for me to reverse my decision. To make matters worse Robert decided to visit that evening and I immediately sent him up to my mother's flat. Michael did not arrive until the evening and I so nearly changed my mind but decided that I must keep to my decision, probably the worst decision I have ever made – although, of course there is no way of knowing how things would have turned out if I had changed my mind.

Over the next few weeks Michael rang me a few times and wanted to see me. Although we managed to meet for coffee in the West End one day, unfortunately mostly the times that he wanted to arrange always coincided with business appointments that I had which I could not rearrange and he understood this to mean that I was not interested. I knew that if I could not meet with him soon the possibility of the relationship continuing was going to be non-existent.

My previous drama coach had contacted me because the drama group were preparing to do a production of

"Blood Wedding" the Garcia Lorca play. He remembered that I had learnt flamenco dancing and asked me if I would go down and choreograph a dance for the cast. I chose Sevillanas which I thought would be easier for non-Spanish dancers to learn and it would be possible to perform it without using castanets. I contacted a guitarist who had worked with my dance teacher Margot. It worked well.

For one of the fashion press shows I had asked David to come along to assist and it was fortunate because one of the model girls did not arrive before the show was due to start so I had to quickly rearrange the whole running order. I asked David to wait outside the showroom so that if the model arrived after the start he could escort her via the back entrance. She arrived part way through the show and when I saw her after the end of the show I was staggered; her photos and at her audition she was very attractive but that morning she looked dreadful. Apparently she had been at a party and I understood smoking hash, it completely ruined her appearance, even if she had arrived on time I would not have been able to use her.

David and I went to Antwerp to visit a publisher and we decided to go by train and ferry. I am not that keen on sea trips but on the outgoing journey, everything was very smooth. We had a meal and the sea was calm so when we returned I was optimistic that all would be well. However, we seated ourselves in the restaurant and were waiting for service when suddenly we started to move out of harbour and everything shot off all the tables. We quickly realized that this was not going to be a good journey. I got up on deck as quickly as possible and stood on deck for the entire journey back to Harwich whilst the deck was almost at 45 degrees, even the crew were having difficulty walking on it. When we finally reached Harwich it took some time for it to be able to dock as it was still so rough. It took a long time for me to agree to another ferry trip although at that time it was necessary if we were going to take a car.

CHAPTER TEN

After a while I did not hear from Michael again and this was very distressing albeit probably as much my fault as Michael's. Unfortunately, I did not have a phone number for him. I concluded that Michael had decided not to try to continue the relationship and I had no way of contacting him; I saw more of Robert which was I suppose very much on the rebound and by the end of March had agreed to marry. The wedding was to take place in June 1968.

We were married at *St Bride's Church* in Fleet Street and the reception was at the International Press Centre which was close by the Church. My girlfriend Marlene met her husband Michael at the reception and they married within the next three months. We only had a few days honeymoon because I was still showing the next season's collections to the press. I recall that I went back to the house after the reception in order to send out press releases to the advertising trade press and the local papers about the wedding!

As my father was not alive to give me away I asked David to perform that duty. Also I decided that I would not wear a full length white dress but I made an A-line coat dress in cream hand woven Rajah Silk teamed with a turban in pale coffee voile - I had ignored an old saying that it is unlucky to make your own wedding dress.

On the eve of the wedding Robert had crashed his car

not seriously but sufficiently to mean that he was unable to use it for the honeymoon and as it was also a bank holiday had been unable to hire a car and, therefore, borrowed a car from his younger brother. This was an exceedingly uncomfortable two-seater open top sports car about which I was less than happy although I am sure that many people would have liked it. We spent a few days in Sussex before returning home whereupon I found out exactly what my new husband was like.

I now discovered that Robert's attitude towards a wife was really that she should be in the kitchen certainly supposed to obey and not have any opinions. Within about six days he hit me for the first time. He informed me that he had paid for the license, paid for the ring and therefore I was his property. In 1968 this was not something that you mentioned to other people, nice ladies did not get hit or certainly did not tell anyone. I had never experienced any kind of physical violence before and did not know anyone else who had, certainly there was never anything of this kind in my family; my father would have been devastated. He was certainly totally unfazed by the fact that my mother was in the house and was even around when this happened. As time went by arguments persisted but I had married in church, taken my vows and divorce could not be considered lightly. From a practical standpoint, I had the complication that my office was in the house, I owned the house and the house was also my mother's home so that there was nowhere to run back to mother.

My cat Honey had always been proprietorial towards me and liked to crawl down inside the bedclothes at night to sleep. Once I was married she did not particularly like my husband and when she heard him locking up she ran upstairs into the bedroom and settled onto his pillow.

In the summer we went on holiday to France and Spain

driving through and en route back we stayed in Paris for a few days. 1968 being the year of the many student disturbances as I returned to the hotel in the afternoon and exited the metro there was a line of French riot police who certainly looked intimidating. We were staying in the Odeon district and whilst getting ready to go out to dinner I noticed that the square was full of police vehicles. We went out to a bistro and found many crowds and riot police all around.

As the autumn went by I was experiencing a considerable number of gynaecological problems not least of which was excessive pain which also caused worse migraines than I normally had. One doctor put me on the pill but after ten days the pain was substantially worse and I was instructed to stop taking the pill. Fortunately I saw another doctor who then sent me to the Royal Free Hospital to be seen by Professor Douglas who was very helpful. It was thought that I had probably had an infection after a very bad bout of glandular fever some years before and they had to clear the fallopian tubes but I was informed that they did not know for how long I would be able to conceive and therefore if I wanted to have a baby I would have to consider that quite quickly. I had never really thought of making a decision about having a baby somehow I had assumed that at some point a pregnancy would take place but I was totally focused on my career.

Following another argument I had to catch a train to go to the West Country for a PR assignment. I had been hired on a freelance basis by a PR agency because one of their clients had a fashion show at a new shop and had to accompany the Sales Director. I met the Sales Director and he drove me to the hotel at which we were staying. He invited me to dinner but – as I thought may happen – he wanted me to go to his room for a drink afterwards. Fortunately, I was able to excuse myself from that and

I hoped he was not too offended. The next morning we went to the shop and they had hired someone with a small lion cub for the show. The cub was adorable but I think that would not get permission nowadays.

Over the next few months I was working very hard on the businesses and we were doing some overseas business trips and by April 1969 I had returned from a trip to Rome when I succumbed to what appeared to be an attack of influenza. About a week before I became ill Michael had phoned me and we had made an arrangement to meet - somehow I had omitted to tell him that I had married in the meantime - Robert was due to be away and I was most certainly looking forward to the meeting. However, Robert's business trip was cancelled, I went down with influenza and then I got a phone call from Michael cancelling our meeting because he was going abroad on a gig. I think I would have got out of bed regardless of the influenza to keep that meeting if Michael had not cancelled. Robert was less than sympathetic that I was ill, complaining that I was ill during his holiday and when he had to go to the pharmacy to get my prescription dispensed demanded the money before he even left the house.

As the days went by I was not recovering and by the Sunday fortunately my mother came in to see me and immediately concluded that I had pneumonia; she called the doctor who came out very quickly and made arrangements for me to go into Coppetts Wood Hospital which was an isolation hospital. By the time I went into hospital I was running such a high fever I really did not know what was going on. Apparently the pneumonia was a viral pneumonia and at that time there was no medication which I could be given, it meant that my body had to fight the infection (hopefully) whilst I lie there.

When my mother and Robert visited me they had to gown-up and be masked. There were windows from the room onto the corridor when meals were delivered the nurses just opened the door, slid the meal onto the tray and departed rapidly. As the fever was reducing I was able to be more aware of the view from the window, there was a beautiful display of rose bushes in the gardens, and also I was getting very claustrophobic being confined. During my stay numerous blood tests were taken and I was told this was because the virus had to be active at the time the blood test was taken in order for it to be identified when analysed. The pneumonia had affected my left lung and there was still some pain on that side. Sometime after I was discharged I was informed that the virus was from birds.

Because of course I was a signatory to the business when my mother visited she often brought paperwork with her that I had to sign. On one occasion when she did not visit Robert brought in some paperwork for my personal accounts which were needed by the accountant. He took this opportunity to have a major argument with me regarding my tax situation and requesting me to let my tax allowance go on to his income; not a good time to have this argument but somehow instinctively I knew that I had to protect myself.

After being in the hospital for a month finally the consultant informed me that I could go home provided that I was completely looked after - as he put it not even having to make a cup of coffee for myself - I was able to confirm that my mother would most definitely be able and more than willing to do those things for me. Then came the day that I was due to go home and early in the morning I felt physically sick and did in fact vomit but there was no way that I was going to tell anyone because I did not want it to stop me going home. When I got home I went straight to bed. A day or so later my mother asked me if I thought I was pregnant because she had noticed that I had been sick each morning - my mother's antenna was unbelievable. I realized that I probably had missed a period.

I went to see the doctor and Robert came with me. It was confirmed that I was pregnant and the doctor told Robert that as I had been very ill I would require a lot of care. Sadly that advice fell on deaf ears.

One Saturday morning there was yet another argument, I went out of the bedroom and it continued on the landing where Robert pushed me. I went down some stairs. Immediately I felt something inside me change. I was very upset and later in the day I noticed some discharge but did not say anything because I really did not want anything to be wrong.

Next morning I was in extreme pain. I called my mother who concluded that I was miscarrying. I was bleeding heavily and before the doctor arrived I lost a foetus. My mother asked if I wished to see it. I looked at it and was amazed at the complete outline of the baby, so clear at such an early stage. When the doctor arrived he arranged for me to be taken into the Royal Free Hospital and called the ambulance. My mother and the doctor saw me into the ambulance. All of this time Robert had been industriously working on decorating the bathroom - a job he had started some six months earlier but until that day shown little interest in finishing. Robert followed the ambulance in his car. Apparently the doctor returned to my mother afterwards and asked if Robert and I got on because he was so surprised at the lack of interest or concern shown by my husband. When I got into hospital the Sister wanted to know where my husband was and a nurse found him outside chatting to the ambulance men.

After a while because I was still in pain, the Sister thought that I could not have lost the baby and I was sent up to theatre. When I returned to the ward I was told that the foetus was removed. So in fact I would have had twins. During the night my blood pressure went down and I had to have a blood transfusion. The next morning I felt very sad and very edgy. I began to realize that I probably would not have had the miscarriage if Robert had not pursued the argument and pushed me. I really felt as though he had killed my babies. When he came to visit I told him that was how I felt and he laughed. I really did not want to go home. The doctor showed his concern by visiting me in hospital.

*Arriving at St. Bride's Church with my Matron of Honour
June 1968*

Arriving at St. Bride's Church with David who will give me away June 1968

CHAPTER ELEVEN

David and I had made a couple of visits to Paris to meet with publishers and David had booked the hotel and we had stayed at the Terrass Hotel in the 18th Arr. which was comfortable. However, on one occasion it was fully booked and he booked another hotel nearby, it was not up to the standard of the Terrass but was acceptable for a night.

At another time I was visiting Paris alone and again could not get into the Terrass so I booked the substitute we had used previously. I arrived very late in the evening with a lot of luggage; a fairly unhelpful Parisian taxi driver was not keen to carry my luggage into the hotel but as I walked in and waited he had to so that he could get paid. I then discovered that there was a female concierge on duty that would not carry my luggage upstairs and the lift was not working. There was a man in the hallway and he offered to take the luggage upstairs. We walked up past the first floor when I noticed a door open and a couple of scantily dressed women standing around and looking very surprised that this man was going past their room and suddenly I realized that I had one of the only two proper hotel rooms in the place - the girls were obviously waiting for their client. I made sure I moved something in front of the door. It reminded of a story a PR friend had told me about a stay she had at a hotel in another country where she had to barricade the door with furniture.

My marriage was not the only problem David, my business partner, was already beginning to drink more than was possibly just social drinking; I had discovered that he was keeping a bottle of Scotch in his desk drawer and although we had, by this time, a secretary working for us I found him tipping Scotch into his coffee. I had known David since we were teenagers and we had a wide group of mutual friends and attended many parties; he was always a fairly heavy drinker to the point that he could become inebriated but this was a different type of drinking.

David had married before I married Robert but that did not stop him staying late in the office and chatting to Robert and having a drink before leaving to go home. Often his wife telephoned and he would arrange to meet her but sometime later was still chatting and drinking; we would remind him that he had told his wife he would meet her, eventually he would leave but must always have been late.

David and I had decided to divide our duties for the company whereby he would deal with sales and accounts and I would deal with sales, public relations and promotion. My mother worked for the company and she dealt with the administration side of orders, invoices and chasing agencies for printing material.

We were very busy with the businesses and I still had some fashion clients for public relations and this of course meant that I rarely finished working at 5.30pm in the evening and therefore was nearly always still in the office when Robert returned home. Robert was totally unable to understand the fact that I had to complete work and that it could not just be left until the next day. The office was based in the house and once I became engrossed in my work I completely forgot anything domestic, therefore, it was not unknown for me to forget to take any food out of the deep freeze; once I was at my desk and working at nine o'clock in the morning I may as well have been a million miles away from the house because I purely concentrated on business. Robert disliked this intensely. There is so often the assumption that when someone works from home they can do household chores in between working but this is a convenient illusion. I realized that Robert had been brought up in a household (he had two brothers) where his mother stopped everything to have dinner on the table for his father in the early evening. Whilst there is nothing wrong with that, my own mother had always prepared dinner for my father but she was not working and she realized the different time pressures that I had with building up the business.

Whilst Robert liked to give people the impression that I did not need to work I was paying the mortgage and all the other major household expenses and he merely gave me housekeeping for food and incidentals even if I had wished to give up my career I could hardly see how there would be any possibility that it would be financially viable. Then of course the house was mine and my mother's home for the rest of her life and therefore I had a responsibility to her.

CHAPTER TWELVE

Robert and I went on holiday in July 1970; we were driving through France and down to Spain. It did not start well as Robert missed the turning exiting the port and could not find the hotel. It was very late at night. Eventually we arrived at the hotel by which time the rather unhelpful owner had already let the room to other guests even though we had the confirmation of the late arrival. We decided to drive on (no other hotels were available). Eventually we stopped and parked up and spent the rest of the night sleeping - or trying to - in the car. Not my idea of a good start to a holiday.

Most of the time I felt physically sick and he kept insisting that I swallow Ivax which was quite revolting and didn't appear to be doing any good. By the time we were in southern Spain I was quite ill one evening and the next morning Robert asked the hotel to recommend a doctor; I saw the doctor later that day and learned that I was, in fact, pregnant. So at least I could stop being forced to take the Ivax and the doctor gave me vitamins and calcium tablets. On the way back to England I had to make a business call in Paris where the publisher took me to lunch and was quite insistent that I ate oysters not a food I like at the best of times.

When I returned to England I saw the gynaecologist and handed them the test results from the Spanish doctor, of course written in Spanish. By this time I was in my early thirties and the hospital regarded this as 'obstetrically ancient'. Not particularly flattering and certainly a slightly different view from the present-day. Six to eight weeks into the pregnancy my blood pressure started to rise and this became a real problem.

Because the problems of thalidomide were very much in the minds of the doctors they were wary about treating high blood pressure with medication specifically for that purpose as they did not know whether there would be any side-effects to the baby. Therefore I was put on phenobarbitone a barbiturate because they considered that as this was such an old established drug there should not be any side-effects. So I spent the next nine months working whilst taking the medication and as the time went by being hospitalized for rest periods where they added a further drug amytal which was supposed to completely sedate me.

The gynaecologist was very co-operative and during one of these enforced rests he let me take an afternoon out to keep appointments at one of the fashion houses much to the astonishment of the ward sister. Even when I went home I was supposed to rest and therefore I would spend quite a lot of the time sitting up in bed surrounded by files of rate cards, dealing with client presentations by telephone until my partner David managed to travel the great distance from Highgate to Islington, just over three miles. David's timekeeping was getting worse and this was very unhelpful.

My swimwear client had a collection to be shown in the autumn. These shows were held at the Grosvenor House Hotel and the client invited all the store buyers as well as press. We always did a photo call for this show but usually the photographers liked to go over into the landscaped area in the middle of Park Lane, this meant a quick dash across the road and over the low railings. I asked Robert to take the day off and accompany me so that he could go with the photographers as I was not quite up to that on this occasion - not surprisingly he was not averse to accompanying bikini clad models.

Naturally for the business bank account both David and I were joint signatories for cheques and other authorizations. However once I was taken into hospital in December 1970 and it was confirmed that I was going to remain there until the birth of my baby I had to sign a number of cheques so that payments could be made even if I was not available at the time. On one occasion I recall that when David visited me he asked for me by my maiden name under which I always worked; from my room I could hear the conversation when David realized and then used my married name. I spent Christmas in the hospital during which time I had developed bronchitis, mainly because the Royal Free Hospital was a very old building and to get patients from the ward over to the diagnostics building meant being taken across an open courtyard in bitterly cold weather.

Just after Christmas it was discovered that my baby had stopped feeding from me and that they would have to induce me; I understand that the bronchial infection made them try to avoid a Caesarean delivery. After about 26 hours in labour my son was finally delivered by forceps along with sedation. I have vague memories of what was going on during that period but the worst thing about it was that when I finally woke up in the middle of the night I found myself in a bed in the middle of the side ward without any ability to be able to call for assistance. I couldn't get out of bed and the bell pull was across the other side of the room. I remember lying there and then hearing people talking outside the door and I thought they were talking about my baby because I heard them say *'well we won't tell her yet'*. And I was so afraid that the baby had died or had some terrible disability that it seemed like ages before I was able to ask anybody. Eventually a nurse came into the room and I asked where my baby was and if he was alive and I was told that he was in an incubator but would be all right.

My husband visited the next morning and he told me that he had seen the baby who was in an incubator and although there were a few little problems nothing to worry about. Later that day I was eventually moved back to my own room and when the doctor came in to see me I asked for more detail about the problems; I was told that the baby had had a one sided fit, a clot of blood on one side of the head and was slightly jaundiced. I was told this was nothing to worry about but to a new mother with all the previous problems it sounded like an enormous amount to worry about.

The day after the delivery my blood pressure returned to normal but it was a short respite as it started to rise again the following day. Because I had been very weak during the latter stages of pregnancy I did not see the baby for several days. Every day I was terrified that something would happen to him. I was in hospital for twelve days after the birth and as by this time my son had regained his birth weight he was able to leave hospital with me. He was quite small only around five and a half pounds.

As I am very superstitious I would not buy anything for the baby before he was born. My mother wanted to knit a shawl and she told me she would have to start that before because otherwise she would not finish it in time. However, as soon as my son was born my mother took my husband to John Lewis and bought a complete set of nappies, clothes, carrycot, pram and all the necessary linen so that it was ready when I got home.

Once I went home I was told I still had to rest as much as possible and of course now I had a baby to look after and a business to run. My blood pressure again raised and I had to make frequent visits to the hospital to have this checked. By April it had not returned to normal and I was transferred to the Cardiology Department for further investigation. Finally I was taken back into hospital for ten days whilst various tests were made the result of which was that although I had high blood pressure there was no treatable reason in other words there was no other illness to be treated. I was prescribed medication to control the blood pressure.

Whilst the gynaecologist had told me that if I wanted to have any more children I should proceed as quickly as possible because they still could not guarantee for how long I would be able to conceive; the doctors treating me for my blood pressure told me that under no circumstances should I become pregnant again and if I did they would have to terminate because my blood pressure would not be able to withstand the strain of another pregnancy.

Naturally I told my husband all of this but he seemed to think that high blood pressure was a matter of one's nerves. When he spoke to his friends on the telephone he would give the impression that he was being very helpful, loving and caring but he would also tell them that it was really just my nerves. My doctor told me that I should be in bed by 9pm in the evening and that my husband would have to get up in the night and do anything else that the baby required after I had gone to bed. This became very stressful because whilst Robert did go into my son and change him over the baby alarm I could hear him telling my son that he was doing it because '*mummy does not want to*'. When this happens on numerous occasions it becomes very distressing.

Because the birth had not been very easy finally with a forceps delivery, I had stitches; and although this had technically healed well it added to the problems of any intimate relations with my husband. He also seemed to totally ignore the fact that it would be dangerous for me to become pregnant again and the discomfort made it impossible for me to use any contraception; because of the high blood pressure I could not use the pill and he flatly refused to use contraception. I was terrified of becoming pregnant and the possibility of a termination; probably more concerned about this than perhaps I would have been had I not had a miscarriage. When I had the miscarriage, I actually saw the first foetus which was about thirteen weeks you could see the outline of the infant and that vision has stayed with me for the rest of my life, so to have a termination would have been devastating for me.

Whilst I was in hospital for the various tests for the blood pressure we had a temporary nanny so now I had to search for the nanny/mother's help and like many mothers in London in the seventies these came and went. Some good, a New Zealand girl who was a kindergarten teacher was one of the early ones and I remembered with pleasure. Some others are probably best forgotten and every now and again including two Norland Nannies made life much easier. However, I only had a daily nanny, Monday-Friday so at 9am I handed over and took my son back at 6pm and weekends.

In the spring of 1971 my son was christened at *St. Brides Church*, Fleet Street; David was his Godfather and Agnes, who had been my Matron of Honour, was Godmother.

I was fortunate that the office was at the house and that my mother had a flat in the house because there is always the morning when the nanny does not show. The day has to be rearranged. Certainly at that time one could not tell clients there was a domestic reason for not being available. Also even if the nanny/mother's help was new at least there were other people in the house to keep an eye on things unlike some mothers I knew who had to leave their child totally alone with the help sometimes with unfortunate outcomes.

When I returned from an appointment one day I went upstairs to take off my coat and my phone rang, it was my secretary asking me to go downstairs immediately as she had just found the mother's help slumped over the fridge. When I got down she had helped her onto the sofa and I discovered a bottle of pills, these appeared to be some type of antidepressant. I could not get much sense out of Susan and I phoned the pharmacy who gave me the contact for the doctor but when I spoke to him he told me to call an ambulance. So off went the mother's help. Late that evening she arrived at the house, it was obvious she was not well but had discharged herself and it was difficult to persuade her that she needed to stay under medical supervision.

David was becoming more and more unreliable. I had discovered that he had used some of the signed cheques for his personal business which was a shock - although I knew his timekeeping had never been good I had always considered he could be trusted. We discussed this and of course he had an explanation. On reflection I suspect that he just had not realized that he was using the wrong cheques. But he was now having more problems with drinking also his marriage had unravelled. He was arriving very late, almost lunch-time some days. However, he did not admit that he had a problem.

One evening I had arranged to have dinner with a girlfriend and I was going to use my husband's car, however, when he arrived home he told me there was a problem with the car. My girlfriend lived in Hampstead and David offered to give me a lift on his way home. It was a terrifying drive, not that far but he was missing other vehicles by inches and when I got to my destination I vowed I would not let David drive me again.

I discovered that David had obtained currency from the bank account without my signature. This was a failing on the part of the bank as they should not have accepted the foreign currency form with just one signature. However, David had his own account at the same branch and obviously the manager had believed whatever explanation David had given for just one signature – or may not even had bothered to enquire.

Things were not going well with my husband, the arguments were getting worse and I was finding it very stressful. On one occasion after a major argument he went out and I phoned his mother to tell her that if he went there I wanted her to keep him there as he had hit me again. She put the phone down on me. A short while later she phoned back and told me she had put down the phone because she was shocked and then I explained but it was a short conversation.

One night at the end of October 1971 we were awoken by an extremely loud explosion. When we investigated we found that it was a bomb in the Post Office Tower, which as the crow flies is a very short distance from the house in Islington. Later we discovered that this was an IRA bomb.

My son's Christening Reception with his Godparents
May 1971

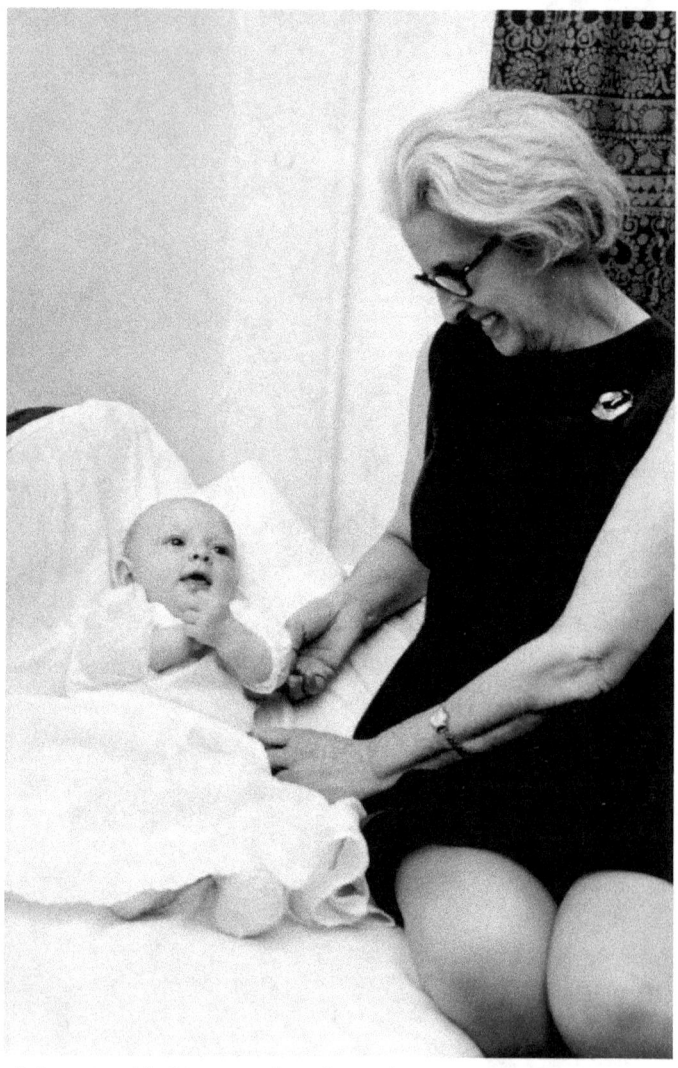

My son with his grandmother Florence Wingham at the Christening Reception May 1971

With my son at the Christening May 1971

With my cat Honey after the Christening May 1971

CHAPTER THIRTEEN

In spring of 1972 I arranged to go to Spain for a combined holiday and business trip and take my son with me with my Danish mother's help. A contact in Spain arranged an apartment for us. My husband had told me he could not come with us and I was pleased because I wanted the time so that I could get plenty of rest and relaxation and, hopefully, build up some strength. However, at the last minute he told me he would accompany us for part of the time. Relaxation went out of the window. The arguments came with us, not the least being the insistence of intimate relations without contraception. When I refused he was extremely abusive to the point that the mother's help could not fail to hear even at the opposite end of the apartment. When I took him to the airport for his return, I heaved a sigh of relief and tried to get some rest.

I knew I would have to make a decision about the marriage because I was having nightmares where I would be running trying to escape from my husband only to wake up and realize it was a dream and my husband was actually beside me in bed. One night he forced me to have sex, only when I considered it years later did I realize that it amounted to rape.

At Whitsun, on the Sunday, during the afternoon the

doorbell rang and my husband answered the door; he came back and told me it was someone for me. I went to the door and nearly fainted, it was Michael. I wanted to grab him and hang on to him. I invited him in and introduced him to my husband and my son. He said he came because he thought there were some items that he had not collected. He said he wanted to play some songs to me and I took a chance and invited him to dinner. My husband was totally unfazed but I warned him that Michael may not return for dinner. However, Michael returned and we had dinner. I learned later that whilst I was putting my son to bed my husband was informing Michael that I had no need to work, that he was able to keep the family and I just worked because I wanted to. Michael left apparently thinking that I had married well.

However, over the next few weeks Michael came to the house a few times during the day and played various songs and talked about the work he had done in Holland including the show '*Hair*' in Amsterdam and a record he had released over there - '*Dust of Time/Because You're There*' via Universal. Apparently he was going back to Holland. From these meetings I knew that the absolutely dead feeling that I had was really down to my relationship with my husband. I actually felt alive during these short meetings with Michael.

He also told me that his mother had informed him that his ex-wife Margaret had committed suicide. I was not entirely surprised by this news because whilst Michael was away Margaret had phoned me to tell me that she had moved into an apartment block but could not sleep and a doctor was due in to give her an injection. The Persian boyfriend she had been seeing at the time of Michael's trial had of course gone back home but had cost her a lot of money. Later she had married and had a baby so it was sad for her that she had taken this action.

During the summer the arguments continued accompanied by the violence and eventually in August there was just one too many and I completely broke down and decided I could not continue with this marriage. I phoned my lawyer friend and asked if he could deal with a divorce. He was horrified and sent me to the hospital to ensure that I was X-rayed. He then suggested meeting me at a friend's flat to discuss the details. He was afraid that my husband may become more violent if he knew I was filing for divorce so he told me not to say anything until he could get the paperwork done to ensure that he moved out. When my husband received these it was the only time in four and a half years that he apologized. The papers arrived and my husband moved out.

My lawyer managed to get the case through quite quickly. When I came out of the Court with my mother and David I had a huge sense of freedom; although I still felt guilty about having to break my marriage vows and go to divorce, the fact that I could go home without the fear and potential of further violence was very liberating.

The only settlement was a very small monthly payment for my son and visiting rights. By the end of the year my divorce came through. It was a great relief but of course another set of problems ensued, the negotiations over visits that must be changed, whether the father will agree to pay towards a school trip. He was only paying £28 a month for my son.

Soon after the divorce I had to go to Paris and Michael came with me so we had a few days there, which was like old times. We travelled out separately and when Michael arrived at the hotel he made what seemed to be a throwaway remake to the effect that he supposed he should marry me now. I didn't really respond because I did not think this was a serious proposal. Years later I often wondered what would have happened if I had pursued this comment and how the years would have unfolded – we'll never know. At this time Michael was sharing David's flat and I had to avoid telling my mother I went to Paris with Michael. When I went to meet with Michael for an evening at David's flat on one occasion my mother kept phoning and made a huge fuss. My mother seemed to be quite happy for me to have the odd evening out with a girlfriend but still did not like me to see Michael.

CHAPTER FOURTEEN

The following year Michael was back in England and started to live with me when he was in London. In January we went to Alicante with my son and the nanny. As it was winter it was very quiet and one evening we went to a nightclub just outside the city. There were not many people in the club and at one point Michael went to the cloakroom; after a while I became concerned and I went to the door only for the doorman to inform me that my friend was outside with the Guardia Civil. I was very apprehensive especially at that time tangling with the Guardia Civil was definitely not a good idea. When I got outside to the car park I found him with two Guardia Civil officers and another man. Some sort of argument was in progress evidently Michael had thought that the other young man had insulted him. I told the Guardia Civil that my friend was a singer, artistic and very temperamental and they suggested I took him home so I grabbed his arm and pulled him to the car and we drove back to the hotel. I warned him to ignore anything else because if he got into trouble with Guardia Civil there would not be much I could - or possibly would - do about it.

The night we returned from Alicante, after I had put my son to bed and was unpacking, Michael came into the bedroom and dropped to his knees, his complexion was ashen. It was obvious he was not well and he admitted he had taken 'something' but would not say what it was. I got him to bed and called an ambulance. When the ambulance arrived the paramedics decided to take him to A & E. I could not go with him because of my son. However, they gave the name of the hospital where he was being taken and suggested when I should phone.

When I telephoned the hospital I suddenly realized that I had no idea which name he would have given. When I spoke to the nurse to enquire I had to summon my best acting skills and said that I did not know if my friend had used one of his stage names, fortunately she said that Johnny Marshall had come in by ambulance and I said *'oh he used that one'* – hoping it was Michael. I had heard him mention a friend by that name.

I asked my mother to babysit whilst I went to collect him. When I arrived at the hospital a nurse spoke with me to say that it was obvious that Michael had taken drugs and I should try to persuade him to refrain from continued use. By this time he was sufficiently recovered to come home. I had never seen him have any bad reaction previously and fortunately did not in the future.

It took a long time for me to realize that the decision I had made at the beginning of 1968 had made him wary of whether I would change my mind. In London once again Pat was working with him on the song writing. Together with another writer Michael had co-written music and sung the title song for the film *'The Wife Swappers'*. I suspected it was an adult movie but it seemed to earn him quite good royalties. Sometimes other musicians would be around rehearsing. He made frequent visits back to Amsterdam then I discovered that he stayed at another woman's house. He had become involved with her when he first went to play in '*Hair*' and she was very devious.

By this time I was making frequent overseas business trips, often with David. Sometimes Michael would come back to London just as I was going away. When in Amsterdam I would see Michael although sometimes these visits were fraught because the woman whose house he stayed at would call my hotel. Sometimes she took his passport so that he could not travel back with me. When he was in Holland it was often difficult to reach him by phone.

Although we represented many travel industry titles there was also a group of major women's magazines from a German publisher within our portfolio. Some of these titles were ideal for upmarket goods such as china and glass. Whenever we contacted the major manufacturers they were always almost pleased to tell us that they were many months late with deliveries, that everyone knew their names and so they did not need to advertise at that time, although it would be different if, and when, we went into the Common Market.

In the run-up to Britain entering the Common Market we did a telephone survey with all the major companies to find out their plans under the new circumstances. However, they still informed us that they were many months late with deliveries; when asked if the customers were prepared to wait the manufacturers were very confident that they would wait. I discovered that another representation company responsible for similar media from France had the exact same experience. It was quite staggering that manufacturers could be so complacent about keeping customers waiting for many months. Not so long after we joined the Common Market several of these large companies were taken over or merged with continental companies. Of course we have now gone full circle after the Referendum so it will be interesting to see how both the trade and advertising changes as well as European travel and whether we will again require international driving licences and extra insurance. We still do not know how the result will affect the country and our shopping habits – all the goods we have become used to buying at home which at one time we could only obtain when abroad.

I was awoken in the night by a noise and thought I should check and went out onto the landing and leaned over the banisters but then could not hear anything so before returning to bed I went to the bathroom, switched on the light which would have shone over the garden, then went back to bed. Next morning my mother came into my room to tell me we had been burgled. She had been downstairs and found that my freezer was opened and there were packs of chicken on the lawn; also my iron had gone. She had already called the police and when they visited they returned my iron. Apparently these burglars had broken into the house next door and stolen a large kitchen knife so presumably had this with them when they were in our house. The police said that they went over the back wall and stole a briefcase but then progressed and took a television which is where they left my iron. I doubt if the owner of the television was as lucky.

1973 saw the onset of the 'three-day-week" which was accompanied by electricity cuts so we had to have candles down in the office but fortunately we had not changed to electric typewriters so could still get work done. My mother was very practical and made sure that we had camping stoves to get my son's food warm if necessary. However, it was a relief when everything went back to normal service.

During this time in the 1970s Michael signed a contract with Les Reed to record a single of some of his own songs - *'Streets Ain't Paved with Gold'/You're Gonna Learn'*.

This was released however Michael was unhappy with the minimal promotion that Les Reed's company gave the single and this led him to return to Amsterdam.

One Sunday when my ex-husband was visiting my son, there was a telephone call; when I answered a man's voice informed me that there was a bomb in the basement. At that time we represented publications from most countries including the Middle East but also I had just fired an Irish girl who had been employed as a mother's help - she had physically slapped my young son so hard that the hand print was still visible when I put him to bed. So I called the police and took my son and my mother out of the house and down the road whilst my ex-husband waited outside the house for the police to arrive. Fortunately, it had been a hoax call but unpleasant nevertheless.

We had installed a telex machine in the office and I decided I should take my father's advice about knowing how to use any equipment in your company so I spent a couple of evenings teaching myself how to use the telex so that I could teach any new staff.

When discussing the songs with Michael I found that he had not joined PRS (Performing Rights Society), he was not very good about protecting his works. I contacted PRS and they sent the membership details but when we sent the list of works we found that most of them had already been registered by his friend Pat, but only in Pat's name. So Pat had to be contacted and all the works had to be re-registered in the joint names. I thought this showed that Pat was not such a good friend as he had never mentioned this omission to Michael.

My son's father visited him one evening a week and Sunday afternoons. But although he made much of his desire to see his son, my ex-husband was not averse to cancelling if he wanted to go out. Also he was quite controlling on visits because if Michael was at the house he would insist that I stay in the same room with him and my son.

One evening when my ex-husband was visiting my son, Michael and David had decided to go to the pub opposite for a drink and I was going to join them. My son felt very grown up if he had some Coca Cola and crisps which actually meant that he got about a thimble full of Coke and half a crisp and the remainder just disappeared into the cupboard. After we had been at the pub for about ten minutes suddenly my ex-husband burst in rather reminiscent of a cowboy entering a saloon and much to the astonishment of the few other patrons. He was raging that we had said that Coke and crisps would be taken back for my son, these were actually already on the bar and he took them and stormed out. After a few minutes I decided to go back and by this time found that he had fed the whole can of Coke and the crisps to my son who was looking decidedly pale. I was appalled at his lack of judgment.

David was interested in starting a media planning company and a friend of his had just left an advertising agency where he worked as a media planner, we started the company with David C running it from nearby offices. This presented certain problems because David started to spend more time at the other office. David C spent some months helping set up but then went to a permanent job. Therefore David decided we should endeavour to keep the media planning company running.

David was becoming more unreliable. At one point he disappeared and was uncontactable for days. We had a major presentation planned for three publishers; we invited around a hundred clients and agency media buyers. The presentations were followed by a reception and normally held in a major central London hotel, usually The Carlton Tower in Knightsbridge. The publishers and guests would all expect both of us to be in attendance but the days passed and I still could not find David. So I hired a private detective to look into his disappearance. Whilst I had to make his excuses at the reception, I soon found out that he had taken his girlfriend to Ireland. It was worrying that the unreliability was getting worse. One day he arrived around lunch-time, totally inebriated, holding onto the table to steady him. By now I was utterly exasperated at his behaviour and told him that if he continued this way, he would ruin the business but his response was *'if I go down so will you'*. I said, *'no, not true'*.

I promptly phoned the Accountant and explained the situation. He reminded me that he had warned against 50/50 partnerships but they prepared the company's accounts and as we still had the media planning consultancy (from which I had resigned my directorship some months previously) the accountants proposed that David relinquished his shares and directorship of the representation company and he received full ownership of the media planning company. He accepted this proposal. However, as that company was running from offices nearby the rent for which was paid by my company, I then had to evict him from the offices which took another six months and lawyer's fees.

After all the legal matters had been resolved I found that David was trying to muddy the waters by sending out letters to the publishers informing them that we had agreed to share the clients; thus I had to contact the publishers to give a fuller explanation and ensure that they did not accept orders from his company. Eventually, I got things back on an even keel but then I discovered that there were problems with the accounts. Over the many months that David had been drinking to excess he had constantly been carrying accounts papers back and forth claiming he was writing them up at home. But in fact there were carrier bags full of invoices which had not been entered and the accountants had to get a qualified bookkeeper to re-write two years accounts. This caused difficulties and was also an expensive exercise. Finally everything was back in order. However, it was a pity that the partnership had been ended because with both of us working on our respective portfolios it would have been so much easier to progress the company.

CHAPTER FIFTEEN

After David's departure the next time I met with the Advertisement Director of the major group of German magazines we represented he expressed concern as to how I would manage without a man as a co-director. He seemed to think that it was only possible for the man to take a client out to lunch. I explained to him that this was an incorrect assumption but it was indicative of this company's attitude at the time.

I had taken on an assistant to help with sales, but he really had difficulty dealing with a wide range of titles at the same time. So I had to make a change. However during his time with us I acquired three more cats; he returned one lunch time with a box containing three very tiny black and white kittens saying he had found the box by his car. I took the kittens and looked after them but I later discovered that he had a black and white cat so I wondered if they were her litter. They ended up with the unoriginal names of Lappy, Smudgy and Fluffy. They were great fun to watch as they frequently acted as a team but a bit difficult to keep track of whilst small with the office using the house.

As we represented many travel titles it was necessary to attend the main travel industry exhibitions including ITB –Berlin, BTL - Portugal, BIT - Italy as well as travel conferences, and these trips were usually combined with additional meetings with publishers and overseas clients which meant I was away a lot of time. My mother was effectively office manager but also supervised whichever nanny was in situ at the time.

The publications we represented came from most European countries and as we had to invoice in the currency of the country we decided it would be more cost effective to have bank accounts in the main currencies. However, at this time it was necessary to obtain Bank of England permission to open such accounts. Our bank made the relevant applications for French Francs, Spanish Pesetas and Dutch Guilders and subsequently we opened accounts in banks in those countries.

However a little later we decided that an account in Deutsche Marks would be useful and again our bank made the request. However, on this occasion it was refused. We requested that the bank re-apply for permission and again it was refused. The bank manager seemed to think that we should just accept this decision; he obviously did not wish to argue our case. So I requested that the bank manager arrange for me to have direct contact with the Bank of England; he seemed incredulous that I would wish to be in direct contact with the Bank. Eventually I obtained the contact and spoke to someone at the Bank and stated my case. Rather grudgingly permission for a meeting was granted but then they phoned me to say that I must take with me either our bank manager or the firm's Accountant. Our bank manager did not wish to accompany me. Therefore I had to request the Accountant from our Auditors to join me at the meeting.

We arrived at the meeting with two members of the Bank's staff. I set out what our company did and the terms of our agreements with publishers, answered their questions and after a while they started to close their files. I was determined we were going to get this permission so I ignored what looked like the end of the meeting and continued to present our case and gradually they started to shuffle papers and open files; I thought I just might be winning. After some more discussion I won the case. It seemed it all hinged on the interpretation of the word 'representative'. I must say that I really begrudged the cost of taking the Accountant because he did absolutely nothing except look very worried when I wouldn't give up.

On one trip to Paris, when I arrived at the last appointment of the day I was greeted with the news that there was an urgent message for me to call the office, when I did it was to learn that my mother had been taken to hospital due to a heart attack. It was too late to get a flight back that evening. But I called the hospital and apparently my mother was comfortable and, they thought her life was not in danger. But this meant that my young son was alone with the mother's help and could have been distressed that I was away and his grandmother had been hospitalized. I called my ex-husband to see if he would visit him and possibly stay at the house that night. He agreed to visit but refused to stay overnight. Eventually, I persuaded my uncle, my mother's brother, and his wife to go to the house and stay the night. I took the next flight back in the morning and went to the hospital. After a couple of weeks in hospital and some convalescence my mother seemed to make a good recovery.

I had always made a point of domestic situations not impinging on business. Ironically, the Monday after I returned to London with my mother in hospital, the nanny had left - work permit problems - and that morning I was starting a new assistant. I spent the day with my son perched on my lap on the seen but not be heard principle whilst I familiarised the assistant with all the titles and dealt with clients. I was also interviewing potential new nannies.

In desperation I started one girl but on the evening of her first day I was confronted by a kitchen full of used utensils - goodness knows what she had cooked. Fortunately, I had a fall-back candidate and I contacted her to start later in the week. At the end of the next day I told the girl that I would have to let her go and my son looked up at her, smiled sweetly and said, *'I told you mummy was going to fire you'*. (It was a forerunner to my son's forthright comments; when his grandmother had recovered and was discussing buying a new bed and replacing her television, my son asked her if it was worthwhile).

Michael was still channel hopping between London and Amsterdam. I had not realized just how much hold Joke had over him in Holland and I found this very distressing. But trying to juggle so much the whole time meant that sometimes I had to put it out of my mind and just concentrate on working and looking after my son.

During the course of working I met various men and some it would have been easy to start a relationship, however, they were all married and I was not prepared to get involved in that type of affair again. Although I nearly got caught on one occasion when I met an expat who worked for an overseas publication; we were abroad at the time and he told me he was divorced and I saw him on a few occasions when attending exhibitions but then found out that although it was true that he was divorced he had omitted to state that he had remarried.

I had offered to try to help Michael organize some auditions and work. But he was very difficult to pin down to keep appointments. Also he had been out of London a lot in the past few years and had lost track of some of the developments, for example the rise in interest of the small theatres even those in pubs where shows were tried out and some well-known actors were working in these venues.

The King's Head Theatre in Islington was founded in 1970 and a production was looking for a singer/actor where Michael completely fitted the description and the producer wanted to audition him. Actually he was quite scathing, suggesting that he didn't work in pubs and it took some persuasion for him to agree. However, he went out that evening with Pat assuring me that he would not forget the audition. During the evening the producer phoned me as he had not arrived and I assured her that he had confirmed he would attend. Of course, I learned that he missed the audition.

On another occasion I secured an audition for him with one of the top West End nightclubs; I was surprised that he seemed very reluctant about it but he went and took a guitarist to accompany him. However, he got quite annoyed when he was kept waiting and it seemed that he was almost trying not to get hired. The club manager auditioned a girl first and that meant he had to wait longer. I asked the guitarist to make sure that he checked the soundtrack and Michael only concentrated on the vocal. The manager spoke to me and asked me to persuade my client to wait patiently. Later I learned that he was really rather nervous about working in nightclubs because many of them were associated with well-known criminals.

It was obvious that he had blown the gig and even more infuriating for me was that when I went to get the car, I brought it round to the stage door, went inside the club to let them know I was outside. Within minutes I went back up to the street and my car was missing. I spoke to a newspaper seller and he said it had been towed away. Because the guitarist had equipment with him I had to put him in a taxi and then phone the police to locate my car. It had been taken to a pound some way away, so another taxi, the cost of retrieving my car from the pound and then a taxi home. Not a good afternoon.

At this time Michael was not actually staying at my house although most of his belongings were still there and he went back to a flat in West London. After I had eventually collected my car from the pound in exchange for a large fine, I went back to the house and checked with the office. However, later I drove over to find this flat in West London. When I got to the address I noticed a car parked which had Dutch number plates. I rang the doorbell and Michael opened it. He seemed a bit surprised to see me but we went upstairs to what seemed to be his room. We made love but I could not suggest staying because I had to get back home for my son.

I got the distinct impression that there was a woman around, little things like cotton pads for make-up removal and so forth. I suspected that maybe Joke was in England especially as the car outside had Dutch number plates. But I couldn't easily find out because Michael was not forthcoming.

Some weeks later, suddenly one evening the doorbell rang and it was Michael arriving in a taxi with various possessions and it looked as though he may have had to leave the West London flat in a hurry. So he was back and we went to bed and made love. It was not easy to get to the bottom of what had been going on. The problem was as it had so often been in the beginning, I became upset and then annoyed when he disappeared but once he was back I virtually melted.

1970s photo-shoot with my son

CHAPTER SIXTEEN

In the mid-seventies I was diagnosed with a lump in my right breast. The hospital was insistent that I cancelled some of my travels and that I entered hospital quickly. The plan was to operate and do a biopsy whilst I was under anaesthetic to determine what surgery they had to do. The Registrar was very concerned.

Before I went in to hospital there was a trip to Amsterdam and I met up with Michael. I told him about the impending surgery and he seemed concerned. We went out to clubs and about 5am we were standing on one of the bridges in Amsterdam and he assured me he would be back in London in time to take me in to hospital. But knowing his dislike of hospitals I was not sure that he would follow through and in the event he did not. I took myself into hospital. I found that the house doctor was totally unprepared to discuss the possible outcome if I had to have the breast removed. She just did not seem able to go in to any detail. The Registrar sounded a little more hopeful when he examined me. The next day I had the surgery; I was very lucky that it was a benign lump.

I had not known what the outcome would be and I had tried to explain to my son that mummy would be very sore when she came home. Although still very young he had taken this on board and was very gentle. A few days after I returned from hospital he asked me if he could touch me and even then he was extremely gentle.

I tried to contact Michael but could not locate him. However, when I called one of the phone numbers a girl called Karen told me that she would tell him that the operation was alright. She said that he had been so worried about the possible outcome. Like so many men he just could not face these difficult situations.

On my next overseas visit I went to Amsterdam and then Paris. Security checks at Amsterdam were always quite thorough, frisked, through the detector frame, hand baggage and so forth. Going through this I was unlucky to be frisked by a very rough female security guard. She slapped my chest with the back of her hand and the pain from my still healing operation was immense. I let out an involuntary yelp and explained what she had done, I gather I had gone ashen and she hustled me with my hand baggage onto the plane. When I met a colleague in Paris apparently I was still as white as a sheet. Later I complained to KLM and was referred to the Dutch police from whom I eventually received an apology.

Six months after the first operation, on a check-up a second lump was found. Fortunately, the hospital was less worried about this one and I was quickly admitted to hospital for another operation. And so another period of healing - a bit wary of airport security checks.

When Michael was back in London, there would be calls from Joke, I found these very distressing. I certainly had not realized just how persistent she would be. He had said that he met her when he was working in *'Hair'*; she worked on costumes and was also a painter. However he frequently assured me that he no longer had a relationship with her, he just stayed at her house. It was hard to know what to believe.

My son was still very young and we went to Holland for a few days taking the nanny and met up with Michael. My son enjoyed the trips to the Zoo and whilst I was working the nanny took him to Madurodam which he enjoyed.

Although Michael was working on songs he was frustrated that there was no real development or financial input. However, during the years that he had been back I had made contact with many publishing and recording companies for him. One company had been interested in *'The Assassin'* although the lyrics did not advocate assassination - quite the contrary - the company got cold feet about the title and so did not proceed to take up a contract; it seemed that an attempted assassination on a high profile individual was still fresh in their minds and they did not want to be seen to promote violence. Another company expressed real interest in a different song which was recorded in the UK but then Michael took the master back to Holland and kept editing and re-editing so that when the tape was again presented the company had gone cold.

One of the conferences I had to attend was the ASTA (American Society of Travel Agents) which on this occasion was being held in Acapulco. The organizers arranged accommodation and I found I was booked into an apartment in a condominium. It was very spacious but although there was a restaurant in the building there was no room service. I hadn't been to Acapulco before and on the drive from the airport realized that parts of the road were quite isolated. Acapulco itself did not appear to have a very developed town; shops were mainly along a strip. All the main events were at the conference centre but some of the more social events were at hotels. When I used taxis I found the vehicles were quite old but also I was a bit wary of some of the drivers. One event was at a hotel located up in the hills on an isolated road. I had looked up the route and watched carefully as we drove to the hotel. I was a bit nervous about a taxi on the return journey. There were a number of Spanish travel people whom I knew and I spoke to a couple who had a rental car and they offered to give me a lift back to the hotel. When we were driving back they told me that if you see anything untoward you just keep going and don't stop.

The weather had been beautiful but on the last day I was sitting on the balcony when suddenly there was a massive wave that came up and over the wall surrounding the pool and it washed all the terrace furniture into the pool. I assumed this had happened before because as I watched the waiters were diving into the pool to retrieve these items. I assumed it would take longer to actually clean the pool which now had a quantity of sand in it.

Michael had been in Holland for quite a while and I had not been in contact with him during that time then I received a phone call from him asking me for a favour. There was a very complicated explanation but the nub of the favour was that he needed a loan. The problem was that I could not see how he was going to be able to repay this loan. Michael told me that Joke had a couple of (apparently) good paintings that she was prepared to sell if absolutely necessary; he was convinced they were worth far more than the loan and told me she would share the funds with him so that he could repay the loan. I wanted to be sure that these paintings were not sold without my knowledge so Michael told me that he would bring them to London. The paintings were going to be left with me on the basis that if the funds were not repaid to me after six months then I could arrange sale of the paintings and refund any monies over and above the loan plus interest.

At Easter holiday I drove over to Amsterdam with my son and Michael had told me he would come back to England. One afternoon there was a phone call for me and Joke told me she had delivered all his belongings to my hotel. I arranged for the porters to pack my car.

Michael arrived at about 5am and then told me he was not going to be able to come back with us. I was upset and furious. He was supposed to be bringing the paintings for me to hold but although he had one for me to take back he could not get the second one. I refused to unpack my car. Michael assured me he would bring the second painting back very soon. So the next day my son and I returned to England with a heavily laden car. Michael returned a couple of weeks later and did have the second painting.

One day I took a phone call from British Airways enquiring if I knew the whereabouts of David. Apparently they had found my name as a previous director of the media-planning company and took a long-shot that I may know where they could locate him. They were most forthcoming and informed me that he had bounced a cheque for a flight to Mexico. I had no idea where he might be and could not help them. Years later I learned from various mutual friends that several of them had received calls from David for help. I was led to believe that he had gone to Mexico with his girlfriend but evidently had run out of money. As I was not in contact with him, I could not verify this information. Although when he contacted me after many years, he had an entirely different version of the event.

CHAPTER SEVENTEEN

In 1979 I had taken my son to Spain on holiday. On returning to the hotel for lunch on the first day the phone rang. It was my accountant to tell me that my mother had had an accident and broken her hip. Apparently she was on the way to an appointment at the ENT hospital in Gray's Inn Road, crossing the road she had to step back and missed her footing on a double kerb. I called the hospital and was told that she had been operated on and was comfortable. I made arrangements for us to travel back to London the following day.

To complicate matters further my cat Honey was ill and my mother had been looking after her so I had to make arrangements for her to be taken into the Vet to be cared for until I returned.

Fortunately, my mother came through the operation well. By the time I arrived at the hospital she was already demanding that they started helping her to walk. I was very concerned because she was in her seventies. However, the hospital said that as she was not overweight and obviously very active there should not be any problems. UCH was very good with her physiotherapy and made sure she could walk up and down the stairs before she was discharged.

By this time my son was at weekly boarding school. I was travelling so much and nanny/mother's help were becoming more difficult to find in London and not necessarily reliable that weekly boarding was a good solution. However, this was the summer holiday period and coming home from holiday early meant that I had to rearrange cover because by this time I had moved the office from home to offices in Kentish Town about two miles away. Some days my son had to go with me to the office and spend the day in the conference room reading or drawing.

During an Easter holiday period my son was signed up for a music course at school and after a couple of days he called me from the bathroom and said he could not get out of the bath. I went in and had to carry him up the stairs to his bedroom. I phoned the doctor who was responsible for the school and drove down to Woodford. After examining my son he made arrangements for me to take him to Great Ormond Street hospital. I drove him to the hospital and after formalities he was admitted.

The hospital did various tests and then one doctor discovered that I was divorced. He seemed to think this was the cause as they had my son running down a corridor. The doctor asked me to get my ex-husband to come to the hospital; I phoned him and he was not very keen but he agreed. I could not see what purpose this was going to serve. The next day we met at the hospital and the doctors arranged to see us in a room with several hospital staff and my son. After a few moments it was obvious that this was upsetting my son and I insisted that he be taken back to the ward.

My ex-husband was making extravagant claims that he would duplicate all his toys at his own house and he could stay there more. Eventually the hospital staff left the room and then my ex-husband reverted to type; he paced up and down the room with the volume and tone of his voice becoming more aggressive. At one point I turned to look at the door and realized that the doctor was looking through a small window. A few minutes later the staff came back in and my ex-husband left.

When I returned to visit my son that evening the Sister was waiting for me with profuse apologies from the doctor for having put me through that ordeal. The hospital decided that my son should see the psychotherapist so for a few weeks I had to collect him from school and take him to these sessions. On one occasion he told me that when he was going to these sessions his legs hurt more than at other times. I told him he should tell the doctor this and subsequently the sessions were cancelled. Later I found that just before the Easter holiday they had played about nine football matches within ten days (the weather had been bad and matches had been cancelled during the term). It was just too much exercise for a ten year old in just such a short space of time.

Not so long after this there were newspaper reports that a father was most keen for his daughter to run in the London marathon and she was deemed too young and there were articles about over-exercise for young children. It seemed to fit what had happened to my son.

My son ensured that we added to our cat family. When I took him back to school one Sunday evening the Matron told me that she understood I was going have Tabitha. I looked at my son for some enlightenment and found that the previous Matron had been fired at half-term and had left her cat in the boarding house. Apparently when this was discovered my son had informed the incoming Matron that his mother would take Tabitha. Not surprisingly she was somewhat nervous; looking at her vaccination card I found that we were her sixth owner.

Michael was still channel hopping. I had hoped that he would settle in London but the pull of Amsterdam seemed magnetic. It was distressing but I just did not know when and how long he would be in London. Sometimes the doorbell would ring early in the morning and it would be Michael - usually asking me to pay the taxi because he had run out of money. He could never tell me how long he would stay and sometimes went back to Amsterdam very quickly others he would stay for several weeks. He was always working on songs and often with his friend Pat.

Towards the end of the seventies he was spending more time back in Holland. He had been disillusioned that he was not getting anywhere with the writing. Also he was disappointed that the contract he had signed with Les Reed's company had not achieved the desired success. Of course, he should have got himself another agent to try for more commercials work and singing gigs but he did not wish to do that. Also he was not very reliable about keeping appointments and therefore agents lose interest fast; it's a crowded profession and there will always be someone else prepared to be more reliable.

Sometimes there were long periods when I neither saw nor spoke with him. When I saw him during one visit to Amsterdam he assured me he would be back soon but although he seemed to find it difficult to tear himself away from the city his life there seemed to be less than good. On one visit I was very surprised that he was talking about taking his life. Apart from the fact that he was a Roman Catholic albeit a bit lapsed, I had never expected to hear him suggest this action. I spent hours talking to him and eventually persuaded him that it was a very bad idea and he promised that he would not take such a step. By the time I left I was reasonably confident that this idea had passed.

CHAPTER EIGHTEEN

I decided I wanted to get the office back into the house and at the beginning 1980 was house hunting again. I briefly looked at properties outside London. One I liked was in Clare in Suffolk, it was in the centre of the town originally it had been a coaching inn and even had a 44 foot drawing room with raised stage - apparently that had been used as a Court room several hundred years before. It had two huge cellars with vaulted ceilings apart from good storage they would have made excellent recording studio space. Unfortunately I could not sell Islington in time so that fell through.

When I looked again eventually I found a house in Highgate, three storey Edwardian. It was owned by an elderly lady but latterly let out in bedsits and the sale was being handled by her daughter. It had a very large garden. I was informed that there was already an offer on the house but that this was subject to planning permission. Following lots of phone calls I managed to secure the house, for once I think an Estate Agent probably earned his commission.

The house needed complete renovation; including central heating, complete rewiring, new bathrooms and decorating throughout and we were moving in at the beginning of January. It was a two-day move and on the second day there was really deep snow. The removal men were a lot faster unloading the second day obviously they worked faster in the snow. The house was freezing. Only one room had heating apart from the electric heaters we had for the bedrooms. Fortunately my son was soon back at school so during the week it only meant heating the bedrooms for my mother and me. But I was certainly wearing more clothes in bed than I could remember ever before.

Within a couple of weeks of moving in I went to Amsterdam and I went straight to the department store and bought a supply of wool tights and vests for myself and my mother. It is the only time I have actually put on more clothes when I got home than I had when I was out.

I had hired a firm of builders who had already estimated for work on the house for the vendor. Builders were not that easy to come by at the time and the vendor gave me a copy of the estimate. I discussed the work including the additional work I wanted and decided to accept the estimate. They were available to start but they wanted to be paid in weekly instalments.

As we were out all day I was worried about our cats getting lost so we left them shut in one room which the builders were not working on at the time with strict instructions that they did not enter. We returned home one evening and could not find the cats; finally we found two huddled into a cupboard and a third under the cupboard but could still not find Lappy. I spent hours out in the garden calling the cat and eventually almost midnight I heard a faint mew and finally found him cowering in a neighbouring garden.

One evening we returned to find the builders had decorated the bay window wall of the kitchen before cutting through the wall to install a door. On another occasion I returned from Berlin to find that they were repainting the toilet before installing the new low suite sanitary ware. Each time the foreman told me not to worry. In fact the foreman's constant refrain was *'don't worry'*. When I came home and found one of the large windows in the dining room was broken, the foreman suggested that the cat had jumped through it.

I decided that I had had enough of this firm especially when the reason for one of these errors was that they did not have anything for that particular workman to do that day.

British Gas was going to install the central heating and I called them to ascertain if they would extend their installation to cover all the plumbing. I then contacted a nearby sanitary wear shop to enquire if they knew a good plumber. As it happened they recommended an Italian and he came and quoted for fitting the bathroom, shower room and other plumbing. He was a good worker. I then found another builder and carpenter and in this way eventually got all the other work finished.

Once I had made the arrangements I sent a letter to the original builders terminating their services. They had been paid to date. Some weeks later I received a letter from Dunn & Bradstreet informing me that the original builder wished to claim breach of contract. When I sent them copies of the correspondence they informed me that under the circumstances they obviously could not continue any action – in fact they suggested that perhaps I should be taking action against the builder.

Unfortunately the move and the extreme cold had obviously adversely affected my mother. One Saturday I took my son out shopping in the morning and when we returned lunch time was surprised to find that my mother was still sitting by the fire and had not had any lunch. She appeared to have signs of chest pains so I called an ambulance and she was taken to Whittington Hospital. We went to the hospital and waited whilst they made some tests and told me that they would keep her in for observation. After some days she was moved to another ward and then was allowed home.

It took until March for the central heating to be completed; the pleasure of warm rooms and hot water for a bath or shower instead of the thimble full of tepid water supplied by the Ascot heater was bliss. The builders were, predictably a nightmare. However, after a variety of builder's blunders and then a change of builders the house was finished and in the autumn I moved the office back into the house.

There was a large black cat at the house and originally I was told that the owners were taking him abroad with them but one day not long before the move they contacted me to ask if I would be prepared to take him over. I agreed although that meant that would bring us up to five cats. The new addition was called Fred and had obviously had to defend his territory but seemed to appreciate being looked after. He had a real character and began to acquiesce to being in at night.

Shortly after we moved my son took entrance exams at his current school and also two in London where he could be a day boy again, fortunately he passed all of them so he went to the one in the City. He much preferred not to be a boarder but of course I still needed a mother's help and firstly had a French girl who proved very good.

I was very interested when I read that Andrew Lloyd-Webber was producing a musical based on T. S. Eliot's "Old Possum's Book of Practical Cats." My son had already been introduced to the T.S. Eliot book and enjoyed the poems so we went to see '*Cats*' soon after it opened. It was an excellent show and the original poems had worked very well.

Over the years negotiating with publishers in various European countries had not always been easy; England had not had a lot of clout and Europeans could be somewhat dismissive. Soon after General Franco of Spain died, there was a strike affecting the airports in Spain and I had to rearrange my appointments. When I met with one hotel director he said that now they were a democracy they too could have strikes - I suggested that it was one part of the democracy they could well do without. However, I noticed after the change of government bringing in the new Prime Minister, Margaret Thatcher, there was a change in attitude overseas. As the time went by even business people who were not necessarily of her political persuasion commented that they wished they had someone like her in their country.

Since moving Michael had not been back to England but I had a phone call from his friend Pat who was in London. I found that Pat wanted me to handle promotion for a girl singer he was trying to promote but he did not seem to have any budget to pay a fee which was not very interesting.

With moving, travelling and a heavy workload I became very tired and one day I was really unwell, when I contacted the doctor who eventually came to see me he diagnosed nervous exhaustion and promptly gave me a massive injection of Valium which seemed to glue me to the bed for about three days. Unfortunately the first day this happened was my son's sports day and I was just not able to attend.

CHAPTER NINETEEN

Late one evening in the summer of 1983 the telephone rang and when I took the call it was Michael. He was in trouble again and wanted me to go to Uxbridge Court the next day. He could not tell me what had happened but I said I would be there. My mother had heard the phone call and told me I did not have to do it but I said that I did and so next morning I took a taxi. It was a lovely summer day and I knew I had to be back home early afternoon to go down to Woodford to collect my son.

When I arrived I located the lawyer dealing with Michael's case and discovered that apparently he had been stupid enough to carry some speed with him when returning to Heathrow and Customs had found it; whilst they accepted it was only sufficient for personal use it was nevertheless illegal. The lawyer said that it would be better for him not to try to get bail because it would be dealt with more quickly. However, the morning dragged on and his case had not been heard. I found the lawyer again and told him I had to go otherwise I would not be able to collect my son. So he went and told Michael who asked for some cigarettes and chocolate. He was given a custodial sentence of a few months.

First he went to Brixton where I visited him. This was the first time I actually saw him. He looked awful. Obviously he had not been looking after himself; I nearly did not recognise him. I told him to use the time to exercise and get himself fit. Shortly he was moved to Pentonville which was easier to visit but just as ghastly. He did at least take the advice to get fit and after a couple of months looked much fitter.

During my conversations with Michael I discovered that, in fact, he had not been returning to England but had been on a train to Germany; when he went through border passport control they discovered his passport was out of date. Therefore, he was returned to Holland and thence to England. So he was only back in England by chance of an out of date passport; he had not been returning to see me. I was unimpressed by this revelation.

Whilst Michael was in Pentonville it came time for me to take my son on our pre-booked holiday. We were going to Gibraltar and then driving into Spain and returning to Gibraltar. Whilst in Gibraltar I decided to take the ferry across to Tangier for the day. Not one of my best planned trips. When we arrived in Tangier I discovered that it was Ramadan. We took a taxi up into the town whilst I tried to remember the various points of interest from my previous stay about twenty years earlier. I received offers of guides and information from one gentleman who's English was very good and who informed me he had lived in Hampstead. However, when I visited previously Tangier was an attractive and vibrant international city, now it looked really down-at-heel. I recalled where the Kasbah had been located and we walked through the town but, of course, that was also closed; one young man offered guiding services but after I politely refused my young son very firmly pointed out that his mother had said *'no thank you'*. It would be fair to say that my son was less than impressed with this trip.

To finish off this less than auspicious trip, when the return ferry left port the sea was no longer millpond calm and I was still seated downstairs and felt very unwell. I went back up on deck and seated myself there. I was feeling quite chilly. The First Officer had been showing my son round the vessel but my son came back and gave me his jacket before continuing his, obviously enjoyable, discovery of the ferry. When we docked at Gibraltar I was feeling quite shaky and expecting to get a taxi back to the hotel. No taxis were available and my son pointed out that we would have to walk. I was exhausted when we reached the hotel.

When Michael was released he came to the house. At this time as delighted as I was to have Michael back at home I could not relax. He still wanted to get the songs recorded but I was not sure enough that he would be reliable to start investing in the recording. He sent me a letter to thank me for having him back this time.

It wasn't long before he started to channel hop between London and Amsterdam. However he was working on the songs and again I found myself staying up into the early hours listening to the songs and then getting up again at 7am and working all day.

I told Michael that if he was living at the house there was to be no cooking in the early hours and then leaving a kitchen full of washing up to greet me in the morning. He did finally organise himself and keep to this.

Of course he still smoked hash. However, when he was young and touring with bands and then through his first marriage he had been prescribed amphetamines. This had been legal and he had been able to continue to get prescriptions up until the early seventies when the law changed. By that time he was psychologically addicted to it and found it easier to obtain in Holland. Also he had made a lot of contacts there and found it easier to get musicians to work with him.

Most of the time that he had been in Holland he had

spent living with (or at the house of) Joke or other women; I already knew he had had a relationship with Joke whilst he was in Holland when he was in '*Hair*' but I had not realized how long. He had told me that the affair had long since been over but she was certainly very difficult. Quite often as soon as he arrived back in England she would start to phone my house to try to reach him. When he was trying to return to England apparently she would take to stealing his passport or some other ploy or cause some sort of trouble.

On one of my overseas visits to Spain and Portugal I had a long trip with several cities involved finally returning from Barcelona; I had a lot of luggage, was very tired and starting a cold. I arrived at the airport early and checked in at the Iberia desk. Suddenly the check-in girl told me I did not have a flight coupon; as there had been several flights I had a few tickets stapled together. There certainly had been a flight coupon when I handed over the ticket. After some argument I demanded to see a supervisor and eventually he arrived. When he saw my ticket together with the Itinerary supplied by Iberia he realized that my ticket was correct so took me to another desk so that they could make out a replacement flight coupon. Around the industry I had heard rumours that they often bumped passengers off flights in order to accommodate staff, but there was no way of knowing if this had been an attempt to do that.

Once I had this I returned to the check-in. By this time there was another staff member on duty who carried out the check-in but as he was dealing with the weight of my baggage the original check-in operative called out '*cuarenta y cuatro* (44kg)'. The check-in operative apologised and said he would have to charge me for all the excess baggage. Having paid the excess baggage charge I then went through security. Yet more problems, I had to open everything and then I was taken to a cubicle and a female security officer proceeded to require me to strip. I had never had this experience before and it seemed neither had the officer and she was just as embarrassed. Finally I got through to airside and was very relieved to board the plane and be on my way.

At New Year Michael went back to Holland and I followed. He wanted to get a flat on his own and we looked at some flats. We found a small flat and he moved in on New Year's Eve. I was at the hotel whilst he went out to try to get some changes to the furniture in the flat. It was approaching midnight and the romantic in me wanted him to return with Champaign on the stroke of twelve. Well, he did return at midnight but sans the Champaign. I suppose that one out of two was better than nothing. The idea of getting a night's sleep was almost impossible. The hotel was on Leidseplein and the revellers were out in force with fireworks and crackers. I had to change the time of my flight because I just had not had enough sleep. Michael wanted me to stay at the flat but, I had to return to London before I could stay there.

Unfortunately shortly after I returned home I was unwell with a rather nasty viral infection. Michael phoned and asked me to go over to Holland but I told him I could not go immediately, he said he understood but obviously thought it was because I did not wish to go. Eventually Michael stayed in Holland for longer periods and was difficult to contact. He had given up the flat which meant that once again he was staying with various people.

I did not hear from Michael and was unable to reach him. When I spoke with the accountant about the earlier loan he advised me to go ahead and sell the paintings that we were holding. So I contacted an auction house and the paintings were sent to them for appraisal and they said they could include them in an upcoming sale. The accountant wrote to Joke to advise her to give her the opportunity to arrange payment of the loan if she wished but she was not prepared to do that so we went ahead with the sale. Not surprisingly although they both sold they realized just about sufficient to cover the original loan.

CHAPTER TWENTY

I returned to the office one day to be given a message for me to call Michael in Holland. When I did I was in for a shock. Everything was very confused but somehow he had been arrested apparently to do with receiving stolen goods. I spoke with the lawyer and told her I really could not believe that and there must be some mistake. After a number of phone calls and correspondence I discovered that all his recording equipment had been confiscated and that he was in jail in Holland. The more conversations I had with the lawyers the more unbelievable the whole thing sounded. Apparently he was also being told that he owed over a hundred thousand guilders in VAT and Tax. This was impossible because he certainly had not been earning sufficient for that volume of tax – or he was being amazingly more successful under yet another pseudonym than I was aware.

In addition to all my other work I had to try to make some sense out of Michael's current predicament. He always believed I could magic away any problem. He wrote me a letter in which he said "…you always knew this day would come…" Well, not really but after all the years little surprised me. After years without any legal problems he seemed to have escalating brushes with the law. Leaving him to his fate would probably have been the most practical solution for me but I knew that if I did not try to assist him he would somehow spiral further down.

I discovered that he had several months sentence to serve but the lawyers told me he would have to leave Holland afterwards and probably would not be allowed to return at least for a while.

I was due to visit Amsterdam for business and I managed to make arrangements to visit him. I had no idea where the jail was but I was informed that as I was coming from overseas I could have two visits in one afternoon; for some bizarre reason that meant a break between the two meetings. I took a taxi from the hotel well actually I walked to the nearest taxi rank being disinclined to ask the hotel to call a taxi to take me to the jail.

I had not seen Michael for some time before this event and so I was a little unsure how to greet him. I did not know if he wished to come back to England to live with me or whether anything had changed.

He told me that his apartment had been raided by the police and that he had been accused of receiving stolen property. I could not ascertain why this would have happened, unless he had badly upset someone and this was some form of payback. Apparently he was taken to the police station and the police had then confiscated all his equipment - recording equipment, drums, guitars, tapes, cameras, everything. They then called in a newspaper and had all the items photographed and it was allowed to appear in the newspaper with a message from the police that anyone recognising their possessions could contact the police. They were not contacted by anyone and eventually agreed to look in the location Michael explained to find the receipts for his possessions. Then they discovered that he did indeed have receipts for all the possessions. So rather than return the possessions to him they called in the Tax Department and the equipment was taken into a warehouse where it stayed under the control of the revenue. Certainly in England this would most likely to have counted as prejudicial to a fair trial but apparently it was not viewed in that way under Dutch legal system.

Michael told me he was writing a rock opera about the events and he spent his time working on it. It was one way of coping with the situation. He was so devastated by these events that he held an enormous amount of hate inside him that his life could have been turned upside down.

In July 1985 Michael was due back but I tried to avoid actually looking forward to his arrival in case he did not come back. However, he duly arrived one morning. I thought that the event as bad as it had been would be put behind him.

This was not to be. He was still incensed by it and very depressed. He still did not have any of his recording equipment and had not found a way of getting the tax department to waive their demands. So I was plunged into masses of correspondence and phone calls to lawyers, the Dutch tax department et al to try to resolve this and get the equipment released and then back to England. I was always very busy and travelling to attend trade fairs in various parts of Europe so this was added workload.

Michael was very busy working on the book of the rock opera *'The Bust'* and working on the songs. He had also written a Christmas song and that was recorded and released *'The Christmas Song – that's why it's Christmas Night'*.

Soon after Michael returned to London we were booked to go on our summer holiday. I had planned that my son and I would stay in Valencia then drive to Puerto

Lumbreras and thence to Nerja. We had planned to stay at the Parador in each of the latter two destinations. As Michael was now in London I encouraged him to join us on the holiday and he agreed.

However, some days into the holiday I began to wonder if it had been a wise decision on my part. Michael was very sulky and did not wish to go out with us; also he was intent on watching television well into the night thus my sleep was disrupted. I had no desire to spoil the holiday for my son so we went out to the beach or sightseeing and if Michael still did not wish to join us we went to dinner. It was hardly how I had envisaged the holiday. However in the last few days when we were in Nerja he suddenly changed his attitude and joined in for the remaining days.

In order that Michael did not have any problems returning to Holland we had consulted a Dutch lawyer. We made arrangements to meet him en route back from Spain. So we routed back through Amsterdam and the next day attended Court in The Hague to arrange his papers to ensure leave to enter and exit the country at will.

We also arranged a meeting at the Tax Department to discuss the excessive tax demand. To be on the safe side I arranged for an interpreter although she was convinced that Michael understood most of the Dutch spoken.

I discussed with Michael whether he planned to knuckle down and work properly before I consulted the accountant regarding investing in the music. It was decided to form a company for publishing and recording and sign Michael to the company. We started using a studio in Highbury where we took a master that was originally recorded in Holland and did some more work on those songs which included *'Sussex County' 'The Assassin', 'Because You're There'*.

With the equipment still in store in Holland, we had to buy a guitar and a four-track, mixing desk and microphone.

After we had returned to England and more correspondence and telephone calls I eventually managed to get the demand reduced from the original 100,000 guilders to 7,500 guilders. Still an unnecessary payment but the best solution we were going to achieve. Because I did not want Michael to throw a spanner in the works I decided to arrange for someone to drive the equipment back to England. However, I had to go over to the tax office and make the payment and then go to their warehouse. When I saw the conditions in which they had kept the instruments and recording equipment I was appalled. It was fortunate that Michael was not there because he would have gone ballistic. I waited while the van was loaded and then flew back home.

The van arrived the day after my return and Michael helped unload. He spent days and days cleaning everything and complaining about the state of the equipment. However, now he had a selection of guitars and the rest of the recording equipment. I had hoped that his mood would lighten with the return of the equipment but he was still very depressed about the past events.

At least he was keeping his word and getting up for the studio bookings we made and working with a sense of purpose.

After Michael had returned and all his instruments and equipment were at the house they were taking up a lot of room in the drawing room but this room I also used for meetings thus it was not very convenient. I decided to build an extension to be used as a studio.

I saw an advertisement in one of the major home and décor magazines and contacted the company. They sent out a representative to survey and give an estimate for the work. After various negotiations we agreed a start date and estimated completion date. I extended my mortgage to cover the cost.

The workmen duly arrived and started to dig for the foundations, however, they did not progress very quickly or efficiently and then they disappeared. This was the beginning of months of correspondence, phone calls and investigations about the company. The company ceased to respond and I contacted the magazine in which they had advertised as obviously it was not good for them to have carried an advertisement for a company that was so unsatisfactory. Eventually after many months a new company took over and, in fact, made a very good job of the extension actually improving on the size and design originally planned.

Whilst working in Holland Michael had worked under the name Jay Dee and then Michael Jay Dee. When we started to release new works I suggested that we use Michael Jay Dean. It was a little confusing for registration of songs with PRS (Performing Rights Society) because they had his real name of Michael Eaton as well as Dean Webb and then the various pseudonyms.

We decided to do a limited release of *'The Christmas Song- that's why it's Christmas Night'*. We hired promotion people and they got some airplay and editorial.

We then changed to a recording studio in Watford. It was a tiny studio but they worked with computers and were able to work on the music. However, Michael was difficult to control once he got to the studio if I did not go to the session. I found that he had recorded a totally different song to that we had agreed for the session, for example *'Rainy Day'*. This may not have been a problem except that on some occasions he decided to work on a song that he had written years before and I subsequently discovered that he had already signed to a publisher. Thus our company could not release it. Conversations with the lawyers ruled it out; well they said if the song did not succeed it probably would not matter but if it did we could end up with a lawsuit.

Of course, during this time Michael was still making quick trips to and from Amsterdam, so if we had anything booked I was always on tenterhooks as to whether he would return to meet the deadline.

On one of my trips to Amsterdam we met up and he told me he was meeting some musicians one of which had a small studio. By late evening he had not returned to the hotel so I went to bed. At around 3am the phone rang, I answered it and it was Michael. He was very excited, they had finished the recording of the title song for '*The Bust*' and he wanted me to go over and listen to it. He gave me an address and phone number. I got dressed and asked the hotel to get me a taxi. The taxi driver took me to the address but when I got to the door it was very dark and there were a number of entry phone buttons and I had no idea which was the correct one. Fortunately the driver had waited to see that I was alright (apparently it was not a very salubrious area). There was a phone box nearby and the driver phoned the number to find out which bell I was supposed to use the driver then walked back with me and waited until Michael came to the door. I listened to the tape and after a while decided we had to leave - I was flying back later that day. Of course, Michael wanted me to pay the studio then but I pointed out that they would have to give me an invoice and we would send the payment. It was about 5am when we got back to the hotel.

By this time my son was now at school in the City and to his relief was a day boy. Mother's helps still came and went although I was lucky with a French girl who stayed for about a year. I then had an Austrian girl whose previous employer's verbal reference was that '*well she didn't kill my children*'. By this time my son was in the CCF at school and he did take a certain pleasure in winding her up as she was anti-war. Fortunately it was all good natured.

By now there was so much going on. I was very busy with my own work but also becoming more and more involved with Michael's. I had very long days because I had to be up by 7am to let the office cleaner in and get my son up and breakfasted before he left for school. Have my own breakfast and be ready for work by 9am. No problem if you go to bed at a reasonable time. But so often Michael would be out late and then I would listen to the songs late into the night. Michael discussed changes he wanted to make (or had made) to some songs and then played the different versions to me. It took several coffees to get me going each morning. Sometimes Michael did not go to bed but there were times when he brought me breakfast in bed and then he went to bed.

My mother was still working in the company but she was now in her eighties so obviously could not do as much as in earlier years. However, she was the one person I had always trusted completely. I knew that even then she could ensure the post was sent, the client's voucher copies and printing material were despatched properly and she could check the petty cash. We had moved over to doing the orders and accounts on the computer so she no longer typed any of these but she was good at chasing the accounts departments to get the payments in.

One day a letter arrived for Michael that had been sent via Equity. He was registered with Equity at my address and his father had written to him and sent the letter to Equity for forwarding. I learned that actually he had not been in touch with his parents for about twelve years. Apparently his mother was unhappy about not knowing where he was but his father had taken the route of writing via Equity and in the letter giving Michael the telephone number of a friend and also a reply envelope with a friend's address so that if Michael did not wish to be in touch his mother would not know. After some days Michael had a telephone conversation with his father. He made an arrangement to visit his parents. I decided not to go with him because although I had met his father once I had never met his mother and I thought that this reunion was something he should do on his own.

When he returned from the visit he told me that during the intervening years his parents had sold their house and moved to America – his sister had lived there for many years. However, apparently this had not worked out well and they moved back to England and had bought a bungalow near Portsmouth.

At a later date we both went to see his parents and I drove us down. We were going to stay overnight. Obviously when his parents had made contact with Michael they had got a single bed for the guest bedroom but as I arrived as well, his mother gave me the bedroom and told Michael he could sleep on the sofa. In the morning Michael brought me a cup of coffee and got into bed with me, it seemed that neither of us had slept well that night.

Conversation was difficult because I had to be very careful what I said as I had no idea how much Michael had told them about the many years they had been out of touch. It was obvious that his mother had not approved of his choice of career. To a great extent this confirmed much that Michael had told me; he believed that once he was no longer on television his mother did not think he was doing anything. Michael had always said that she blamed his father for signing the permission for his contracts when he was young.

CHAPTER TWENTY-ONE

In late 1986 my mother became unwell and was diagnosed with shingles. It was very painful as it went across the head. She was unwell for a few weeks. It seemed to take some time for her to recover and she obviously was not able to carry on in the office as previously. We had employed a junior to deal with post and various jobs however she nearly drove me to distraction when I discovered she could not spell and was unreliable. We had a messenger who took the post and did deliveries to agencies.

Sometime after my mother had recovered from shingles it seemed that she was having problems with her memory. We consulted the doctor who diagnosed her with 'patchy dementia' but did not offer much in the way of advice or help. After a few months I again took her to the doctor and asked for a second opinion. We saw a consultant in Harley Street. She gave a similar diagnosis but prescribed a very low dose of medication to help her to be less agitated. Of course by this time my mother could no longer work in the office but did not really know how to occupy the time. In the early stages it seemed that she only confused which day of the week it was and similar things. Sometimes she would look through magazines and ask about different clients remembering which clients we had booked previously and enquiring what had happened to their advertising.

One evening in March 1987 I switched on the news to see the pictures showing the sinking of the Herald of Free Enterprise, the ferry which sank just after leaving the Belgian port of Zeebrugge, Michael walked into the room as the news was unfolding. I was so thankful that he was in London at the time because otherwise I would have been very worried in case he had been on board - he used various routes for travel. They spoke about the possibility of the bow doors being left open and Michael said he had seen that on ferries he had travelled on.

In November of the same year the news was full of the Kings Cross underground fire and I was relieved that my son was already home. Highgate was on the Northern Line tube and he should not have had to change at Kings Cross however sometimes he used different routes some of which took him into Kings Cross so I was even more thankful that he had arrived home before the event.

So by now I felt as though I needed to split myself into about four different people. My son was now in his teens and tended to prefer to stay in his bedroom. Michael was intermittently still depressed and stayed in the bedroom when not working, my mother needed my attention and just for good measure I had a full day's work to do and clients to deal with not to mention the various freelance staff.

Now in addition to having a mother's help I started to have a carer for my mother. On one occasion a repeat prescription for the medication had had to be obtained whilst I was away and the new supply started to be used just before my return. I returned late in the day and went to see my mother and found she had left the cooker hob on, so I turned it off and talked to her but she said she was fine and was going to bed soon. Up until now she had been cooking for herself and generally looking after herself apart from some part time help. I was very tired and unpacked and went to bed.

Next morning I got my son off to school, got ready and then went upstairs to see my mother before going into the office. To my horror I found her curled up on her kitchen floor. After the first shock I called my cleaner who had just arrived and asked her to help me get my mother into her bedroom. She was beginning to wake up and we got her into a chair and gave her some tea. I called the doctor but, of course, could only leave a message with the receptionist for someone to call back. I decided it was probably not useful to take her to A& E as by now she was ready to eat. My cleaner stayed with her whilst I started work.

I called the agency I had used previously and fortunately the Australian girl who worked with my mother a while back was available and she came in later that day. Later she looked at the medication and at the bottle from the previous supply and came to see me to tell me that the latest supply was much stronger. I called the pharmacy but they said that as the first prescription was a private one they did not have a copy to compare it with but confirmed they had dispensed according to the latest prescription from the doctor. I called the doctor again and had great difficulty getting a clear answer as to what had happened. I decided that we would stop that medication. The dementia was definitely more obvious after this event. From then on it was necessary to have a regular carer from morning to early evening.

Later the doctor suggested that at some point I would have to consider a nursing home and recommended one in Highgate. He suggested that we put my mother's name down so she was on the waiting list. The matron came to see her and in some ways she seemed to quite like the idea. For the remainder of the year we continued at home. However, as the year went by there was considerable deterioration. She started to wander about the house at night going into the other bedrooms. This was difficult because she would disturb my son or come into my room and wake me up. I was also worried that she might fall on the stairs. When Michael was in London he often worked through the night and then he would hear her on the stairs and take her back to her room.

My son had signed up for a parachute course with the army and heart in mouth I had agreed. So whilst he was away I was on tenterhooks about his safety. Michael had promised he would not leave London until I heard from my son that he had jumped and was safe. Two ladies who worked for me each had young sons and each day they asked me *'has he jumped yet'*. I was relieved when I received the phone call from my highly delighted son to tell me he had jumped and all was well.

By spring 1988 I was exhausted and the doctor told me that if I did not get my mother into the nursing home soon I would end up in hospital. My son and Michael both encouraged me to take the step for the sake of my health. I was very reluctant to take that final step to put her in the nursing home but eventually that step was taken in May 1988.

At first she was given her own room but as the weeks went by she was moved to a double room. She changed completely; when I visited she refused to speak to me. When I visited with my son she flatly refused to acknowledge me. She said her daughter would not have put her into the nursing home. My son was very firm with her and told her that if she did not speak to me he would leave and she finally acknowledged me. But I noticed that she seemed to have lost weight.

One day in the summer I had a call to say that my mother was not eating. I was very surprised because before she went into the home she had a very good appetite. I visited that day and the residents were in the lounge having tea. It took me nearly three quarters of an hour to get her to eat one fairy cake. I realized that she was having trouble swallowing and remembered that our own doctor had told me at an earlier time that some drugs used contracted the muscles of the throat but the home had assured me that they would not medicate her. I found the matron and finally got her to admit that they were giving my mother medication. Further questioning elicited the details of the medication. I called my doctor but he told me that another doctor in the practice was responsible for the nursing home patients and eventually I got them to stop the medication. By now she was very thin and also I discovered that they had removed her dentures with which she had never had any problems.

A few weeks later in August 1988 I received a call to say that my mother was not well. I went to the nursing home with my son and Michael. I found my mother in a ward with a screen round her. She was not fully conscious. After a short while I told my son that he could go and see his friend. Michael stayed with me and the staff told me that my mother was now dying. Michael and I stayed until very late and the staff suggested that as we were only a few minutes' drive away there was no point in staying longer and they would call me. We went back to the house and went to bed although I did not sleep.

A few hours later the phone rang and the nursing home told me to go back. Michael came with me but my son was asleep and I made the decision not to wake him. When we got back it was obvious that it was just a matter of waiting. Then I thought it was the end and called the staff and my mother breathed her last. I was very upset especially I already felt guilty about placing her in the nursing home and I had lost my mother. It was around 5am and the staff made me coffee because I had to drive and then we went home. I had to wake my son and tell him his grandmother had passed away.

I had to contact both my mother's brothers and let them know the funeral arrangements. I decided that the funeral would be in Chingford because when my father died my mother had arranged that the plot would be for both of them. Eventually my uncle and aunt who lived near London attended but her brother who lived in the Midlands decided that he could not travel into London. Michael kept his word and did not take off to Holland whilst I was dealing with this and attended the funeral with me and was very supportive.

Apart from the obvious sadness at the loss of my mother, I had already missed the conversations I used to have with her before she became ill. When I was travelling I would always speak to her each day and catch up on anything with my son but also on any queries in the office. On my return from trips she was interested in how my meetings had gone, whether I had met new publishers and how any queries had been resolved during my visits. She was also always interested if I had bought any clothes or anything for my son. Also if I went to the theatre she was always interested to know if it was good, if I enjoyed the performance. For some time this had been missing and now my mother had died there was no one close with whom I could have the same conversations. My mother had been very interested in the progress of the business and had met a number of the publishers and clients when we held the presentations. After all these years I still find that I miss being able to discuss matters with her.

I had been very dissatisfied with the way the nursing home had looked after my mother. They had expressly disregarded the matter of medication and not discussed it with me before proceeding to give her tablets that appeared to reduce her ability to eat. I was seriously considering gathering the relevant information to sue the home; however, as events unfolded over the next few months, that had to be put on hold.

CHAPTER TWENTY-TWO

Michael had another brush with the law by returning from Holland via Dover. He had brought with him some speed for his own use. Apparently an officer on duty when he was detained at Heathrow happened to be at Dover so of course recognised him and had a search done. I had a phone call from him. He was released on bail but had to go back down to Dover for the hearing. Fortunately, he just got a fine. I asked why he took such chances but he said he did not know anywhere in London to get it that he could trust. Once again I tried to encourage him to give up the drugs. The NHS clinics for addiction apparently did not cover amphetamine use and the private clinics cost around £7,500. He did attend a few sessions at a group counselling clinic once a week but he was not very impressed and it did not seem to make much difference.

The end of one afternoon I suddenly had the feeling that Michael was off to Holland. He should not leave the country because he had not yet paid the fine and if he did not pay it by the due date of course he would have a further problem. I knew if he went to Holland without making the payment he may not get back in time to make the payment. I was furious and jumped in the car to drive to Victoria Coach station to see if I could find him before he left. When I got there everyone was coming out of the building but I went in and was told that it was closing because of a bomb scare. So I went back home. Later Michael came in but did not say where he had been.

The following day I guessed he would try again, so I went down to Victoria Coach station again and this time caught him boarding the bus. By this time I had discovered that he had withdrawn money he should have used for the fine. He was determined to continue with his journey and I slapped his face and stormed off. I was very angry but also upset.

As the days went by I realized I was going to have difficulty in locating him and also to get him back in time to pay the fine. By this time we had already invested money in recordings and therefore if he overstayed and did not pay the fine there were likely to be further legal problems. In the event he had not returned in time and our accountant advised me that it would be cheaper for me to make the payment because of the investment already made. Eventually I reached Michael and he gave me the date he would be back in England.

On many occasions when Michael had been in Holland and it seemed so difficult to pin down when he would return I had resorted to praying for Divine intervention to perhaps get him to change and stop making these trips to Holland. Or at least return when he said he would. Overall it was distressing to have him spend time there and on one occasion suddenly I felt very calm and hoped that maybe my prayers had been answered. But one time when he had guaranteed to me he would be back the next day and did not arrive I just flipped and went to the wardrobe, pulled out some of his favourite shirts and chopped off a sleeve here and there and left them in a heap. He returned the next day when he found them he was quite rueful; in many ways he accepted consequences.

I decided that we should exhibit at the *Midem* music festival in Cannes. So we booked the stand and then had to arrange the promotion material and music we needed to be able to promote the works. *Midem* was held in January so just before I went to the travel fair *Fitur* in Madrid. The organizers recommended a bilingual receptionist for stand work. She was very helpful as she had worked on *Midem* before and lived locally in Cannes. I wanted to stay at one of the hotels close to the centre to save much travelling between the hotel and the fair. The arrangements for hotels were made via the fair organizers and we were allocated a hotel on the Croisette. Of course Michael was not going to be at the fair early in the morning. Fortunately with *Midem* the organizers arranged all the furniture for the stand including telephone and audio equipment. Consequently it was possible to arrive on the first day and start to work. Barbara our stand help was very good. She knew her way around the venue and helped me to contact the press to arrange interviews. I had already arranged an editorial in the *Midem* daily news and this brought some people to the stand.

One evening there was a major performance at the conference centre and all exhibitors had tickets to attend. When we arrived there were long queues and the security staff were not entirely helpful in the way they admitted the guests. Suddenly Michael became really irritated and decided he did not wish to wait. He just gave one of tickets to me and started to walk away. When I looked at the ticket I realized that it was his ticket as they were all named and identified with the exhibitor badges. I had to try to catch up with him. By the time I did there was no chance of getting back into the show. Eventually we got back to the hotel and the evening finished with a very late dinner in bed.

I visited other exhibitors to organize appointments for publishers and recording companies to listen to tapes.

As my mother had died we no longer required a house affording a separate flat for her. Also by autumn 1988 the clients were requesting information faxed to them rather than being sent round by messenger. I concluded that it might now be the time to sell the London house and move outside; it would reduce costs and I could release some of the equity in the house to invest in the music.

I came across an ad for a house in Suffolk, timber framed with two acres of ground and outbuildings. Outbuildings immediately indicated room for office and studio use. I liked the sound of this property and phoned the agent to arrange a viewing for the following Saturday.

I asked Michael if he wished to go with me and he agreed. I asked my son, but he did not wish to get up early on the Saturday morning and, I suspect, thought it was one of mother's projects. So Michael and I drove up to Suffolk in late October. It was a small town with the Grade II listed property about 300 hundred years old just at the end of the main road. We went in and the wood burner was roaring away, it seemed very warm and cosy. The outbuildings, one of which was the original forge building, would allow for my office and a separate studio. Also there was a good sized laundry room and cloakroom. There was a large garden, two paddocks and stables/barns; so lots of storage area. I explained it to my son on my return but he was less than interested. About a week later I went back to view for a second time and again asked my son if he wished to go with me but he had other arrangements

The following week I was at World Travel Market exhibition; we had our own stand with a number of publishers participating so it was very busy. However, I had decided to buy and was dealing with the negotiation.

I had a call to say that my offer was accepted and so instructed the solicitors. My son was quite surprised when I told him that my offer had been accepted. It was already November and I had more travelling to do so I decided not to put the London house on the market until the New Year.

After Christmas I placed the London house on the market. I told the agents they would have to make all appointments and deal with all viewings. They took a large ad in the local paper and had a viewing the next day.

In retrospect and probably if I had not been so busy and I had more time to consider the matter, it would have been possible to convert the house into two apartments and build another house in the grounds thus still living in London – hindsight is such a wonderful thing.

CHAPTER TWENTY-THREE

Early in the New Year of 1989 Michael suddenly haemorrhaged. He lost a lot of blood and I called an ambulance. He was taken to Whittington Hospital. Once he was seen by a doctor they made an appointment for some tests and for him to be seen by the urology consultant. He was then allowed home. The next day we went back for him to have the tests. When he saw the Registrar I told Michael he would have to tell the doctors the substances that he was taking. We were also shortly due to go to *Midem* and they said Michael could go but they made an appointment for him to go into hospital for tests under anaesthetic on his return.

I took Michael to hospital in the morning he was due to have an examination under anaesthetic but early afternoon I had a phone call from him asking me to collect him. Apparently he had been bounced off the list and told he could go home. I was annoyed and told him he should have tried to stay to see if they could put him on the list for the next day. But he was already dressed and waiting at the entrance so I drove round to collect him.

The next morning I phoned the hospital to arrange another appointment. That came about a week later and this time I took him up to the ward and waited until the doctor came to see him. I asked that he definitely go to theatre because we could not make other studio arrangements if these appointments kept being changed; I was also concerned that if there were too many delays he may decide to go to Holland and that could seriously interrupt hospital appointments. Fortunately he did go to theatre that day and when I went back to see him the doctor came to the ward and discussed the results. Unfortunately they were not good. The examination and tests had shown that there was cancer in the bladder.

We had another outpatient appointment where they discussed the options. The hospital wanted to start treatment with chemotherapy and I took him for the sessions. The doctor was very concerned that Michael should stop smoking. Every time we went for his treatment the doctor would ask me about the smoking and I said that he was finding it very difficult to stop.

There was some improvement in Michael's condition and the hospital was hopeful that the chemotherapy may have worked. They said if he had to have radiotherapy he would be transferred to The Royal Free Hospital in Hampstead.

By now I had signed the contract on the Suffolk house with an extended completion date - it fortunately suited both me and the vendor. It would also only leave one term for my son at school in London before he finished. I assumed that I would be able to arrange accommodation for him for that time.

The plan was to sell London and buy in Suffolk but also to buy a studio flat in London to use for working and when we needed to stay in London. I looked at several studio flats but did not immediately find anything suitable. However, the buyer of my house was going to convert the house into a kindergarten but as they were not using the top floor immediately they offered it to me to rent.

It was obviously a very busy time. Selling a house is

always time consuming but with Michael's illness as well as trade fairs and continuing with recording for Michael there was no free time at all.

Because of Michael's health I decided to cancel a visit to a trade fair in Berlin in the March. The Advertisement Director of one of the German titles we represented phoned as soon as she was back in her office to berate me for not attending the fair. My contracts did not require me to attend these fairs and the publishers did not make any financial contribution towards the cost of attendance. Therefore attending was entirely at my discretion. Going to the trade fairs was very useful which is why I attended so many but to miss one was hardly a disaster.

The move was planned for the end of April. So there was much to do as work had to continue right up to moving day and commence as soon as we got to Suffolk. I had to travel to Suffolk a number of times to make arrangements with builders, heating, telephones and other building work. Originally the vendor had agreed to some work on the outbuildings being started before completion however she proved less co-operative than hoped and frequently would not let the builders gain entrance. I planned to use the original forge building for the office, but one room had a WW2 gun emplacement, solid reinforced concrete and I expected that we could remove it. However, I was informed that as the house was Grade II listed I could not have it removed. Obviously the gun emplacement was not there when the building was originally built but it was in place when the property was listed. So I had to have a desk built around the gun emplacement.

The removal companies all calculated it as a three day move; on the final day it went on incredibly late in the evening before everything was finally loaded. I was driving up with Michael and all five cats plus some clothes and my son was driving up with his friend and various personal items. We had arranged to stay at a hotel in the town that night and I had to contact the owner to let them know we would be very late. When we arrived and got the cats settled in the room we finally got to bed. But before that we had to keep a lookout for my son so that he did not wake the owner again.

In the morning my son and his friend got to the house first and met the removal crew. I took the cats down to the house in the carriers and as it was a beautiful day we set the carrier baskets under the chestnut tree so they had good shade but fresh air. Finally all the household goods were in the house but there were many boxes with magazines and papers stacked in the courtyard. We were so lucky with the weather being fine and dry. It was well into the evening and my son and his friend went to look for the nearest 7/11 or other late night shop, they drove quite a way before finding anything but eventually came back with some food. Suddenly we all realized we were no longer in London and a quick trip for forgotten groceries in the evening may not be possible.

The vendor had refused to let the British Gas engineers test the central heating system. Of course once in we realized why - it didn't work! The central heating boiler was in the laundry room which was an outbuilding across the courtyard from the house. Unfortunately this meant that all the piping had been run under the flagstones in the courtyard. British Gas informed me that the boiler was not up to standard and therefore we would have to have a new boiler so eventually this was located on the patio next to the kitchen.

Michael always believed that there was another chance with everything and I knew he was still smoking. An appointment was made for him to see the oncologist at the Royal Free. It was decided that they could offer thirty sessions of radiotherapy, this meant five sessions a week for six weeks. They said that this was the maximum that could be given.

By now we had moved to Suffolk and the Royal Free offered to transfer Michael to a more local hospital but I knew that they had a good reputation and said we would get him to London. As he was quite strong and did not need constant nursing they made arrangements for him to stay at a Marie Curie nursing home close to the hospital for the week nights. This meant that almost as soon as we had moved at the end of April, the treatment started in May and I drove him down to the hospital on a Monday and then came back. Drove down again on the Wednesday to see him and back and then went to collect him on the Friday. It was extremely tiring.

In general he did not seem to have many side effects from the radiotherapy. However on one occasion when I telephoned the Marie Curie home to check they had just sent him into hospital because he had developed severe pain. I contacted the hospital and went down the next morning.

When I arrived he was asking for more pain killers. I checked with the nursing staff and found they had given him morphine, not a drug he liked. After a while I was able to speak with a doctor and found they were reluctant to give him further doses because they had seen from his notes that he had taken drugs. I pointed out that if they did not give him something there was every chance he would get out of the hospital and go and find something. I then had to stay with him and finally sit on his shoulders to keep him in bed.

Fortunately my son arrived and he went to the cafeteria and brought some refreshments back to the ward to keep me going. After a while he left and I stayed to ensure Michael was given the medication. I was at the hospital for several hours not returning home to Suffolk until late evening. I was exhausted and went to bed. Normally he would have been coming home the next day but I assumed that he would still be in hospital. Not so, I received a telephone call from him around mid-morning asking what time I was going to collect him. He sounded fit and healthy and I was still trying to wake up. Unfortunately, once he was feeling fit he assumed that I must be as well with very little concept of how tiring it was to keep driving back and forth.

During the treatment time Michael was still working on the songs. If it had been any singer signed to a company I would have told him to wait until treatment was completed but throughout the treatment before we moved he had been into the studio but I knew he needed something to give him hope for the future.

One day I collected him from the hospital in Hampstead and then we went to collect Maurice, the guitarist, and drove to the studio in Watford. Just as we were leaving the slip road from the M1 my car stopped. Michael had no idea about the mechanics of cars and neither apparently did the guitarist. Fortunately another motorist stopped and came to my aid. He seemed to think the cam belt had gone. He offered to drive me to a nearby pub where there was a phone. I called the AA and then called the studio because the longer we were stuck we were losing studio hours and I had to get Michael back to hospital. John from the studio came and collected Michael and Maurice and the instruments and took me back to the car

Eventually one of the AA sub-contractors came and I arranged for them to take me to the studio. Then I arranged for the AA to relay my car up to Suffolk the next day. I had to call my son to come and collect me and then take Michael back to hospital and get Maurice back into London and, eventually take us back to Suffolk. After that I made sure I had a phone fitted in my car. I decided that if I was going to be driving alone I wanted to have the security of easy communication.

CHAPTER TWENTY-FOUR

During the summer, we arranged for a couple of videos to be made. One for *'The Christmas Song'* and the other for *'You can be his hero but - first you've gotta be dead'* which was based on John Lennon's murder. For the Christmas song we decided to use the house as location. We had difficulty getting a Christmas tree in August but eventually we got one and dressed the tree. Then had a roaring fire in the open fireplace and closed the curtains. It was a very hot day and absolutely roasting in the room. But we got the recording. Then we recorded the other song. Firstly, we did a folk version in the grounds of the house. There was a stream running round the garden and we used the bridge and other parts of the garden for this version. Later we made a rock version in Southend-on-Sea. The video company decided to use the pier (part of which was still burned out).

Michael – photo-shoot for 'Streets Ain't Paved with Gold' This track is on 'Best of Michael Eaton' – digital album – Amazon and other streaming services.

Michael – photo-shoot for 'You Can be his Hero' This track is on 'Best of Michael Eaton' – digital album – Amazon and other streaming services.

I had still been concerned that Michael was secretly smoking and I tried to impress on him that there could not be any more radiotherapy and was very upset. Finally he said he would stop because he had seen how much it upset me.

One day in September I was in my office and he called me to say that he had haemorrhaged again. This was very bad news. I called the oncologist's secretary at the Royal Free Hospital and she made arrangements for me to take Michael to hospital within a couple of days. We drove down and he was seen very quickly. The oncologist arranged for him to be admitted to hospital immediately. The hospital did more tests and there were discussions with the urology consultant. Finally, Michael was informed that they could operate to remove the bladder and if the cancer had not gone anywhere else there was a very good chance of a complete recovery. So the arrangements for surgery were made for some days later.

In the meantime he had decided to ask to see a Roman Catholic priest. I was pleased that he had made this decision.

Up until a few days before the surgery Michael's parents had still not been informed of his illness. He had only been back in contact with them over the last couple of years and he always had the opinion that it was better not to tell them bad news. However, I thought they should know he was due to have major surgery and told him I would inform his father. I phoned his father and explained the situation. He said that he would not tell Michael's mother until they had news about the result.

I stayed in the nearby hotel. He was going to surgery early in the morning and my son came down so we both went in to see him before going into surgery. The day went very slowly. Eventually the time arrived when I could phone the hospital for news. I was told that he was through surgery and that they got all the cancer. He was in ICU but I could see him around 6 pm. So we went to the hospital. My son did not go into the ward because he had a cough. I went in and Michael was hooked up to a variety of tubes. I was told I could visit again the next day.

I stayed in London again and for several days until Michael was more stable on the high dependency section of the ward. After a few days when he was now able to talk he told me that he loved me and that we would get married when he was fit and he added that he wouldn't go back on his word. I was delighted and phoned my son to tell him.

Gradually Michael went from high dependency to a side room. The stoma nurse came in to see him to teach him how to use the stoma bag and how to change it. Jokingly he said that was alright because I would do it for him but the nurse told him he would not go home until he could do it himself. This rapidly focused his mind on the instruction.

As he was progressing with recovery his parents came to visit him. During the visit he told his mother that we were going to be married and she said it was about time. She took off her rings and told him to choose one to give me as an engagement ring.

He was still in hospital at the beginning of November and we watched fireworks across London from the window of his room, the hospital is very high and there was an excellent view across London.

Soon afterwards Michael returned home. We had to be careful about his diet but quite soon he was able to eat quite well.

In mid-November I had to attend World Travel Market in London; we had a stand at the exhibition and my son was working at the exhibition with me. I was concerned about Michael being on his own during that time so I asked his father to come and stay with him.

Earlier in the year, when we thought that the treatment had been successful, we had re-booked for *Midem* for January 1990. By the autumn it was too late to cancel or, if we did, we would not be able to get any refund. But Michael said that he could manage to get to the fair. We had arranged vinyl singles of several songs, some from '*The Bust*' and included '*She Don't Worry*', '*Mr Electricity*', '*Demon Doll*', '*Sun Brushed my Eyes*' so that we could use them as promos.

Fortunately Michael had a strong constitution and physically was having a good recovery, although he was having more problems with the psychological aspect of recovery. We did not have very long to get ready for *Midem* but I continued to prepare everything.

In January 1990 we went to *Midem*. We arranged distribution of some of the singles and although Michael was not very strong yet I arranged some press interviews. He worked hard to deal with them especially as he was not supported by any substances.

At the end of the fair we were waiting in the hotel lobby for the taxi when I took a phone call from my son. He was phoning to tell us that the weather in England was getting very bad, storms similar to the 1987 storms apparently. Certainly all the flags along the Croisette were blowing about. When we got to the airport there were some delays and when we boarded the plane the Air France stewards were quite agitated about the weather. In order to speed the turnaround time for the plane it was being hot refuelled. However, it was a reasonably smooth journey back to Heathrow. As we came through customs there was a Tannoy message for me; when I took the call it was from by son. Apparently the wind blowing around our courtyard had thrown various objects around and broken a window cutting him quite badly. We could not drive up to Suffolk that night and so we stayed at the flat in London. Next day we drove back home. One of the paddocks was flooded and the swans were swimming on it as if it was a lake and the stream was swollen right up the bank.

Michael had periodic check-ups with the hospital and also saw the GP. The GP had referred him for counselling sessions to help with not smoking and also staying off amphetamines. He seemed to think that the counselling helped.

Michael was still working on the rock opera and other songs and we went back into the studio.

We had not yet married because Michael wanted to be sure he would be well enough. However, in the summer a date was decided for August 1990. I asked my son to organise the car and a cake. My girlfriend suggested the function room at St.Etheldreda's Church in Holborn, London and they arranged the catering for the reception. It is an historic Church and the oldest Catholic Church in England. We made arrangements for the marriage to be at the Rosebery Avenue Register office which was not far from St. Etheldreda's.

In order not to tempt fate I did not make the dress for this wedding. I went into London and took a quick trip round some department stores. I was not looking for a bridal dress but wanted something special. I found a two-piece in ivory chiffon over silk and embroidered with tiny beads. I quickly found a hat in ivory. To accessorize I teemed cream leather sling-back heels and a small beaded clutch bag.

I decided that we should not stay together the night before and therefore arranged two hotels. I drove down alone to the Marriott in Hampstead and my son drove down with Michael to another hotel nearby. I made sure that Michael and my son shared a room and that my son took responsibility to get him to the Register office at the right time. It all worked very smoothly.

During the reception I told my girlfriend that we wanted to arrange a Blessing and she rushed off to find Father Charles. She came back and told me she had given him a précis for the last quarter of a century and he had immediately agreed telling her it was a marriage made in Heaven. The church is beautiful and we were so delighted to have the Blessing there. I really thought that now we may have many years together after all the events of the past years.

During the Autumn Michael was quite depressed as he had not really taken on board that the consultant had told him that the operation was very likely to make him impotent. He was put in touch with one of the self-help groups of patients for similar surgery. Because of his background in music they gave him the name of another fellow who apparently had similar interests. Over the next weeks this fellow Mick came down to see Michael. Michael took him to the studio and played some of his music. I don't think Michael found it especially helpful except that he could discuss the problems with another man with the same experience.

Some weeks later we drove to Peterborough to see Mick at his home with some other friends. They told him about a charity concert they were organising for New Year's Eve in aid of the Macmillan Nurses. Mick offered to get Michael a slot in the concert so that he could perform some of his songs. We met Owen who was organizing the event.

A week or so later we went to Owen's house and they discussed the songs for the concert. Originally they were offering him a slot for three songs but ultimately this came down to one song and that he would have to use a backing track. I think Michael was beginning to have second thoughts about this event. He was advised to use the backing track as they could not guarantee that any of the groups, who were mostly performing tributes of sixties numbers, would necessarily perform his music. However, using a backing track relies upon the engineer giving the sound level the singer wishes. Michael asked me to stay with the engineer to check on this but the engineer did not greatly appreciate the oversight.

As the concert was in Peterborough we all had to go and stay overnight. My son and his girlfriend and their friends came with us. I had to arrange for someone to look after all the cats whilst we were away.

The concert was in a huge marquee which was freezing cold although they were using heaters to try to warm it up. It was full. There were several groups performing. However, as Michael was performing alone he had to use a backing track. The evening went off alright although Michael was not very happy about the volume used for his set also he had been scheduled as the last set thus bringing him close to the midnight deadline. We stayed overnight at a hotel but there was one low point for me when Michael called me by the name of his first wife. This was very surprising as in all the years I had known him this was the first time it had happened.

We drove back home the following day. Later that day Michael was somewhat unhappy and told me that at the end of the show he had seen one of the organizers giving cash to several of the groups; as the show was for charity we had assumed we bore all expenses. The next day Mick phoned and we raised this matter with him and he admitted that they had paid expenses, so we submitted our expenses and these were paid.

August 1990 – Outside Register Office in Rosebery Avenue.

ANOTHER LOOK AT LIFE

Michael with Maurice the guitarist at the Reception 1990

CHAPTER TWENTY-FIVE

Shortly after New Year Michael developed a cough and what appeared to be a cold. It was unusual for him to get respiratory illnesses. I called the doctor in and because of the cancer history she sent him to the local hospital for an X-ray. The day we went it was heavy snow which made the half hour drive really nasty. After the X-ray we were asked to wait for him to see a doctor. When the consultant saw us he told Michael that the X-ray showed that he had lung cancer. The consultant was not very tactful in the way he delivered the news and Michael was very shaken by the news. So was I. They decided to admit Michael into hospital straight away. I phoned my son to let him know that Michael was staying in hospital so it would be a while before I got back.

My son and I went back to see Michael that evening but we did not learn very much more.

The next day I phoned the Royal Free and spoke to the oncologist's secretary and they made an appointment for him to be seen in London. The local hospital had not given any hope so it was worth a second opinion.

He was only in the local hospital for a few days but when I left one evening to walk back to my car it really hit me that I was going to lose him and I was overwhelmed with grief. I was sobbing all the way back to the car and had trouble pulling myself together to drive home.

Soon afterwards we went into London. The hospital did various tests and X-rays were taken. After further consultations the specialist told Michael that they thought they could operate but that they could not be certain they could get the cancer.

We had returned home and Michael was given morphine to help the pain. This time he realized that it was a very serious situation. In some ways I don't think he wanted to have the surgery but on the other hand I think he felt that he should go ahead in case it proved successful.

He had seen a well-known faith healer on television and asked me to contact her. I sent her a letter but when she eventually replied it was to send a list of all her tapes, literature and books. However, we were put in contact with a faith healer who lived quite close by and I took Michael to see her on a couple of occasions and she came to the house on another occasion. Mick whom he had met from the support association suggested another healer whom they said was supposed to be very good. They arranged to drive him down to the house and undertake a session. I was very sceptical about the benefits of these healers but I went along with it because it seemed to give Michael another line of hope.

Michael spent a lot of time dictating lyrics for songs he had written long ago but never finalised. He was hoping that it would give me something to work with. He also dictated a scenario for a promotion in case he pulled through and we could use it for publicity. It was difficult for the typist to transcribe the tapes because his voice was very faint.

It became obvious that if he did not pull through this latest cancer I would be left with reels of recording tapes, masters and scripts which I would have to hope I would be able to exploit; he had done so much work in the last few years that to have this illness bring his life to an end so soon seemed so unlucky albeit he had wasted a number of years at an earlier time.

In the March we were given the date to take him back to the hospital to prepare for the surgery. He was in hospital a few days before the surgery. One day when I was at the hospital the SHO told me that it was now doubtful they could get the cancer because it looked as if it had gone into the wall of the chest. However, we decided that it was his only chance to go ahead with the operation.

We were at the hospital on the morning that he was going to surgery and saw him before he was taken down to theatre.

Again I stayed at the nearby hotel and had to wait all morning and until early afternoon before I could telephone. I waited and then made the call but this time all the nursing staff would tell me was that he was back on the ward and that I could visit later. When I asked about the result they would only tell me that I must speak to the doctor later. I just knew it was bad news because with the previous operation they were so pleased to tell me that the operation had been a success. I phoned my son and told him of my fears. Later I went to the hospital, this time Michael was in a side room with tubes and drains. I went to speak to him and then asked to see the doctor. The consultant was not at the hospital but I saw his Registrar. The Registrar told me that they could not get the tumour the cancer had penetrated the wall of the chest. It was the end of the line, no more chances. I asked the Registrar if this meant that the original cancer had returned but was told no that this was completely different and he would have had this even if he had not had the bladder cancer. I asked the Registrar how long my husband had to live and was told months not years. So I hoped for many months.

He told me that they had not told Michael the result so I had to return to his bedside and realized that I would have to find the right time to tell him.

I sat by the bedside all evening. He couldn't talk very much. It was very late in the evening but he did not want me to leave. I found a nurse and asked if I could have a pillow and blanket because he wanted me to stay. Finally, he was settled enough for me to leave around 6am; I returned to the hotel and went to bed. I was absolutely exhausted both physically and emotionally.

When we married the previous August I had thought that after all the years with so many separations for various reasons we may now have the opportunity for a lengthy marriage - it was even possible we could celebrate a silver wedding. How wrong could I be?

The next day I visited again and this time Michael was more awake and eventually he asked me what the doctors had told me. I had to tell him that they could not remove the tumour and it was months, not years. I tried to be very positive and say that maybe it could be at least eleven months, maybe they could be wrong and it could be longer. I just had to take a deep breath and walk on stage and be as cheerful as possible.

I stayed in London for several days so I could see him each day and spend as much time as possible particularly whilst he was coming to terms with the news.

Privately I was devastated but could not let Michael see how upset I was. So for every visit I made sure that I kept up my usual appearance and tried not to look as though I had been crying.

The hospital talked about palliative care and even said that they may try radiotherapy to endeavour to relieve the pain. After a while they got the Pain Consultant to see him and he was given an injection to try to relieve some of the pain.

He saw the priest in hospital and I was very pleased about that and hoped that it helped. He was talking about going to Lourdes and also trying to explore faith healing. The priest told him it could be difficult for me because he probably was not strong enough to walk and that could mean me pushing him in a hospital bed. Mick and his friend came to the hospital to see Michael and then they again brought the faith healer in to see him.

By now Michael had been moved to a single room and I spent as much time as possible visiting. However, I was still working and having to drive to and from Suffolk. It could be frustrating when phoning the hospital in the morning to be told he had a comfortable night when, in fact, I knew he had been in pain.

He started to ask about coming home. I spoke to the Sister about this and I was a little surprised that she said that they were not encouraging that idea.

One evening I got back late after visiting and my son told me that Mick and his friend had phoned and wanted me to phone back. Although I was very tired I phoned them and they told me that Michael wanted to come home - which I already knew. Apparently he had asked them whether they could arrange to put a mattress in a transit van and drive him home. I was furious and very tired but tried to patiently explain that the problem was that he may require medical care en route and this was causing the delay, also that the hospital was not very keen to discharge him.

Eventually, the hospital agreed that he could come home and they arranged for an ambulance to drive him up to Suffolk. He arrived quite early in the morning and the crew took him upstairs to make sure that he was safely in bed. Shortly after he arrived he started to feel sick. The journey had obviously been a strain. I called the doctor and she came out to see him. He came home on 17 April.

My son and his girlfriend were at the house. Eventually I went to bed trying not to disturb Michael as he seemed to be asleep. I could hear various sounds in the ceiling and I had my suspicions that there might be mice. Suddenly I turned over in bed and put my hand down to my handbag at the side of the bed only for a mouse to run across. Being totally petrified of them I had an automatic reaction and screamed and jumped up across the bed and onto the landing. My poor husband reacted and got up, by this time my son was out on the landing; apparently he thought that Michael must have died but was somewhat dismissive when he realized it was a mouse. My husband took my handbag and emptied it out into the bath - of course the mouse had long since disappeared. The whole episode had a kind of black humour. Hardly the most tranquil first night at home for my husband. The next day I called in the pest control people. We still had three cats but they were all very elderly and had long since given up hunting.

A few days later my son wanted to go into London because it was his girlfriend's birthday and I agreed. The district nurse came in each day and I got her to stay with Michael whilst I showered and got ready. Then I was alone and became very worried. I really did not know what to expect, it had seemed that everyone was expecting an early end. I was very exhausted and quite scared. On the Saturday evening Michael was frequently trying to be sick and I called the GP. The duty doctor said he would come out and arrived quite late. Not very tactful he said that he had another call but that one had already gone. He left me in no doubt that my husband would die very soon. I was so relieved to see my son when he returned on Sunday, just to have someone else in the house.

I talked to Michael about making contact with the local priest and he said he would like to see him but wanted me to call as he was not up to making the telephone call. So I contacted Father Brendan and he agreed to come and see him once I assured him the request actually came from Michael.

After Michael had been home for about a week the doctor asked if Michael had told his parents and I said that he had told me not to tell them. She was quite shocked and told me that I was to call them; as it happened his father telephoned that day so I told him and he made arrangements to come and see Michael.

I had always had the ability to go onto auto-pilot to deal with work regardless of what was happening in my personal life and never was it more essential than during this period of Michael's illness. Close to the end the doctor was with Michael and I had to take a call whilst in the bedroom and without thinking switched to complete business mode and then reverted to the rather more emotional conversation I had been having with the doctor.

By now the district nurse was coming in each day and the doctor visited most days. It was suggested that I contact the Macmillan Nurses. When I did I was told the amount of cover they normally offered. However, as Michael was not expected to have very long to live what I wanted was twenty four hour cover for the last period. Eventually I managed to make this arrangement.

My son had asked his friend to come and stay at 'the end'. I suddenly realized that if Michael died at home I would have to arrange for the funeral directors to collect him from home. We were still very new to the town and had no idea of all the services. Eventually my son and his friend consulted Yellow Pages and commenced phoning several different funeral directors to ascertain which had a 24-hour service that could collect the deceased from home. Of course, they were asked where the person was and they had to say that the person in question was still alive - again a somewhat black humour moment as they felt that it sounded that they were planning to dispose of someone.

Michael was on a morphine pump for the pain and it was now giving the pain relief that was needed.

Much to the inconvenience of the district nurses Michael had decided to take himself up to the bedroom on the second floor because he thought the bed might be more comfortable.

Eric, Michael's father, arrived around 25 April but his mother did not make the journey. That night the nurse said that the end was very close and we called the priest Father Brendan who came as soon as possible. Just prior to the arrival of Father Brendan Michael suddenly decided to come down to our bedroom but sat on the stairs and he took off his wedding ring and placed it on my finger.

The duty doctor arrived but this was not the doctor who had been looking after Michael and he seemed intent on telling me that I could cry; I became really cross with him as I knew that I was controlling myself and really did not need him or anyone else to tell me I could cry – there would be plenty of time for that later. I think my son and, indeed, Michael's father, thought that I was having a problem with this doctor and he was ushered out.

When the priest arrived my son made him some coffee and the priest although perfectly competent had obviously been imbibing the vino. He arrived at nearly midnight and stayed for several hours and I was eternally grateful to him because he helped me enormously. In the early hours of the morning Michael was still holding onto life and the priest left. So we went through another day and at the end of the evening the nurse told me I should get some rest but that she would call me. It was not long before she came to get me and Eric and I and my son were all with Michael when he breathed his last.

The doctor was called and the nurse went into action

to prepare Michael. I went downstairs and waited. The doctor was still there when the funeral directors arrived. At this point I departed to another room; I preferred to remember Michael in the bedroom than to have a memory of his removal from the house. Eventually I went to bed in my son's room but was not feeling well and the nurse came and sat with me for some while which I found very helpful.

The next morning Eric left to go back home and he came and thanked me for all that I had done for Michael.

Once I got up I knew I had to go into the bedroom so walked straight in to find that the nurse had left the curtains open and the bed was stripped.

My son's friend was still at the house and they suggested going to lunch at the pub and I thought this a good idea as I wasn't quite sure last time I had a meal and certainly would not be cooking. After we finished my son's friend left and my son and I went back to the house. I got some other bedding and went to bed. Fortunately I was so exhausted that I fell asleep.

The next few days were taken up with making the funeral arrangements, contacting people and going to see the cemetery. On one morning both the Rector from the Parish Church arrived to see me at almost the same time as the Priest, although I found that the Rector seemed to find it difficult to find anything to say to me. The Priest suggested the small graveyard at Withermarsh and my son drove me there. It was a very restful, small graveyard in the countryside and I felt that it would be perfect. There was a very small church alongside where the service could be held.

The church did not have an organ or even a piano so my son's friend, an organist, arranged some music with a keyboard. Michael's parents both came for the funeral as well as various friends. His parents stayed that night and went home the next day.

During these very difficult times my son who was only twenty had been very reliable, certainly proved his organizational abilities and shown traces of his maternal grandfather's sense of duty.

Now the words of Father Charles, when he spoke to my friend to arrange the Blessing back in August, seemed very prophetic when he told her it was 'A Marriage Made in Heaven'. Within such a short time it was obviously the only place that it may really take place, even if delayed by some years.

CHAPTER TWENTY-SIX

The previous few years had been very fraught and exhausting; running my business, my mother had had dementia and a few months after her death Michael developed bladder cancer. We had moved to Suffolk just after my husband's diagnosis and I spent many hours driving between Suffolk and London. There must have been an angel on my shoulder because some nights when I drove back I was so tired I had to drive with the window down to keep awake.

However, I went straight back to work after the funeral; when you work for yourself there is little else you can do you have to keep going. In any case I always believe that work is the best therapy. At least when you are mentally occupied you cannot think of anything else.

The GP had suggested bereavement counselling but my view was that no-one could bring my husband back therefore the counselling would have very little to offer. I know that some people find this helpful but I considered work to be better.

The night before my husband died he sat on the stairs and took off his wedding ring and placed it on my finger. Although we had known each for a quarter of a century we had only married eight months earlier following his recovery from the first cancer. Sadly he had now succumbed to a second but terminal cancer.

I wore the ring from that time on but one Sunday a few weeks after the funeral on my return from visiting the grave I suddenly noticed it was missing. I was inconsolable. I asked my son to revisit the grave with me to see if I had lost it there but it was not to be found.

On the Monday morning I telephoned the Editor of a magazine specializing in treasure hunting and metal detecting. I explained the problem and asked if she could direct me to anywhere it was possible just to hire the equipment. She very kindly gave me the name of a shop some miles away and my son drove over to collect the metal detector.

In the meantime I hunted through the house again and again. I even tipped everything out of the wheelie bin – not a task I would have done for anything else – but to no avail. I was getting more upset as the time went by.

We went all over the garden including the very large grassed area where I had parked my car, again without success.

My son returned with the metal detector and used it over all the garden area again and also revisited the grave but still no success.

I was desperate to find the ring; it meant an enormous amount to me especially so early in the bereavement.

Finally in the afternoon I asked my son to return to the grave with me and try again. On that occasion I walked to the end of the graveyard where some of the old graves were located because I remembered that I had looked at those on the previous day. Suddenly the sun came out and as I looked down I saw something glinting – it was the ring. I was absolutely overwhelmed with relief.

I immediately put the ring away safely and next day went to the jewellers to have it re-sized.

When I telephoned the Editor of the magazine to thank her for her help she informed me that she had previously had a similar enquiry from a man whose fiancé had ended the engagement whilst they were driving around the M25 and she had thrown the ring out of the car.

So when my husband died I was exhausted but had carried on working. The first Gulf War had a detrimental effect on travel advertising and thus reduced business for the titles we represented. A number of very well-known airlines, hotel chains and car rental companies had instructed their staff to reduce travel to certain areas; some had cut routes during the war and took time to reintroduce the routes, thus adding to the overall recession of the early 1990s.

One Saturday very soon after the funeral I was alone in the kitchen preparing to feed the cats and I could hear lots of noises in the ceiling above and realized the mouse must have gained a family – it sounded more like a rugger match – in spite of the pest control visit. I picked up a copy of Yellow Pages and found another company which claimed a 24-hour service. I telephoned and was given an appointment for early on the Sunday morning. I decided I could not stand another night of wondering if a mouse would appear in my bedroom so I phoned a nearby hotel, booked myself in for the night. I cooked dinner then ensured the cats were settled and drove to the hotel. With relief I went to bed and slept. Next morning I drove back and the owner of the new pest control company informed me that the previous company should have used open bait in the loft. He carried out the necessary service and said that I should not have any more problems after a few days. He was right and ever since I have had a service from that company in each house I have lived in. It is preventative I have no desire to host any uninvited visitors.

Shortly after Michael died, one evening in the summer I let Fred - by now a very elderly cat - into the garden where he normally spent a very short time but after a while I was concerned that he had not returned and I went into the garden to look for him, calling him and suddenly I heard a very low yowl and then I saw that he had rolled down the bank and was in the stream, holding his head up in some reeds.

I scrambled down the bank and picked him up and got him indoors. He was soaking wet almost the water could be wrung out. I wrapped him in towels and phoned the Vet whilst trying to dry him. Then with him still wrapped in towels I ran down the road to the Vets and they examined him and gave him injections and said that only overnight would tell if he would recover. Fred had a lot of stamina and was a cat that definitely wanted to live. I placed him on a towel on my bed and sat up all night watching him. Fortunately he got through the night and I took him back to the Vet next morning where he had more injections. Slowly he recovered.

I noticed that in the last weeks when Michael was ill it was very busy with telephone calls from friends, doctors and nurses in and out. Immediately after his death again people telephoned and there was much to do. However, some weeks after the funeral I noticed that phone calls were fewer and indeed when girlfriends phoned some seemed almost unwilling to speak about Michael I think that in that situation they were afraid that I may become emotional and they wouldn't know what to say. As time went by I found that some girlfriends started to ask if there was a new man in my life. I was emotionally drained and the thought of another relationship was more than I could contemplate.

We had rented a serviced office in North London where our Accountant worked and one week my son was taking paperwork down there. I got a call from my son to say there was a small problem, furry and eight legs actually two very small kittens. He found them when he was driving down a road where some houses were being demolished. One was in the road and he thought too young to be out so he stopped to investigate and followed the kitten back to the building site where he found another kitten curled up with the mother but the mother had obviously been in an RTA and was dead.

After making enquiries he could not find anyone wishing to own the kittens so he got a box from a nearby newsagent and put them in the car. So we suddenly owned two more cats. They were very pretty one was brown spotted tabby and her sister a grey striped tabby. I named them Marilise and Maribel. I think our elderly cats found these two a bit frisky for them.

During this time my girlfriend Rosemary informed me that she was finally going to marry her long-time partner Billy, however as Billy was a Roman Catholic priest this relationship had of course had many difficulties. Now Billy had retired apart from broadcasting and writing it was more possible for him to make the necessary application to the Vatican for permission. They booked the church but she told me they were still awaiting the final permission. She invited my son and me to the wedding. It was in a church in North London and they had many guests but at the crucial part of the ceremony when the priest pronounces the couple are 'man and wife' we noticed that did not happen. At the reception Rosemary told me that they were still awaiting the relevant paperwork. A few weeks later Rosemary told me they would have a civil ceremony but it was at the same Register Office where Michael and I married in August 1990 so she was concerned that I might find it upsetting, however, I thought it would be alright. Therefore, we went to the Register Office ceremony and Rosemary asked me to be a Witness. This went well and we all had lunch at a nearby restaurant. A couple of months or so later they actually received the permission and Rosemary decided they would have another ceremony in church – so for someone who had not married until she was in her 50s she had three weddings in the space of a few months.

My son was working with me at this time as viral pleurisy had stopped him taking up the flying career he had planned.

Many advertising agencies were preparing plans for their clients on the off-chance that the clients would release a budget but usually to no avail.

I closed the publishing and recording company we had launched for my husband's music as it was uneconomic for me to continue to inject funds without anyone to work on the music or lyrics to exploit the works.

However, I enrolled for a weekend course on writing a musical which was very interesting and gave me the information that would be required to present the manuscript for the rock opera *'The Bust'*. I knew it would be very difficult to even get this work-shopped without injecting more funds. However, I thought that it would be worthwhile to have it set-up correctly to be able to present if an opportunity arose.

Maureen Wingham – early 1990s photo-shoot

Flamenco Course Jerez

CHAPTER TWENTY-SEVEN

Shortly before my husband had passed away my godfather died and thus my aunt was now a widow. We had never been especially close however I invited her for the weekend. I had met my first husband at her son's – my cousin –wedding. During our conversations my aunt told me that when her son heard that I was going to marry his friend he had asked her if I knew what he was like. Apparently he had a reputation for being aggressive and settling an argument with violence. I was very surprised and thought that it would have been nice if someone had told me that twenty odd years before. I might have been able to avoid all the problems of my first marriage.

I had the opportunity to pitch for a low budget PR account for a theatre but it meant driving several hundred miles for the meeting. I left home late morning and planned to stay overnight for the meeting next morning. Before I left home I felt slightly sick however did not pay too much attention to that as I considered it was probably the prospect of a long drive and the pitch the following day. Half way up the motorway I was suddenly very sick; I felt absolutely awful. Of course the sensible course of action would probably have been to take the next exit and return home. But I did not want to miss the appointment so I carried on. I phoned my son (I had a fixed phone in my car) and told him what had happened and eventually he stayed on the speaker and gave me directions right to the door of the hotel.

He had already phoned the hotel to tell them I was en route but that I was not very well. When I arrived I got a large bottle of mineral water and spent the night very still and drinking water. Next morning I kept the appointment, did the presentation and then drove home. On the drive back I was surprised and concerned to note that the route near to the destination was on fairly narrow roads with steep drops; last night it had been very misty so in a way I was pleased I had not known about the type of road then. I asked my son to wait until I got home and when I did I went straight to bed and my son left to go away for the weekend.

Unfortunately the next day I was due to collect my aunt again to stay the weekend. However, next morning I felt absolutely terrible, I did not have any energy, all my limbs ached. I called the doctor for a home visit. In the meantime I had contacted someone who was driving from London up to my office and arranged for her to collect my aunt. Of course, it would really have been more sensible to ask my aunt if she minded if we re-scheduled the visit.

The doctor arrived just after my aunt and the doctor said she had been waiting for this to happen to me. She said that she knew everything would catch up with me sooner or later. The doctor turned to my aunt and suggested she could look after me but that fell very much on deaf ears. Finally I hauled myself out of bed and went down to make coffee and a sandwich for my aunt. I really could have done without a guest. Normally I could have a coffee and get myself together. But whatever this was it was not going to go with a few cups of coffee. Entertaining my aunt was an effort. At one point she ran her finger over one of the bookshelves and muttered something about a duster. Sympathy and empathy were definitely not on offer. Eventually my son returned on the Sunday and I had to ask him to drive my aunt back home.

As the weeks went by the diagnosis was variously chronic fatigue syndrome, post viral syndrome and then ME. As there was no treatment regardless of the name attached to the condition it did not really make much difference. The doctor was convinced it was the result of everything that had been happening over the last few years and only time would improve the situation.

For a long time I found it very difficult to get out of bed – not usual for me even when I have been ill. I did a lot of work whilst in bed going into the office later in the day but of course dealing with client calls regardless. Driving into London took a lot of energy but I still did that as necessary.

Part of my work involved visiting trade fairs. These are naturally very tiring even when you are fit but with the ME it was very difficult. For the overseas fairs it meant visiting the fair in the morning and then having to rest in the hotel in the afternoon, I just could not spend as much time walking around as usual. When I returned home it also meant having to rest.

A new trade fair started in 1993 this was the Arabian Travel Market and it was in Dubai. We had some clients emanating from the region so I decided to go to the fair. To ensure I got full benefit from the visit I went to Dubai but spent a day in Kuwait to see an agency working with us and then a day to Bahrain to see agencies.

The taxi journey from the airport to the agency in Kuwait was a bit hairy – although I had directions (and a map) when we got close to the address the driver seemed very unsure and I told him to stop and I would get out. I spoke to a man standing outside a nearby shop and he phoned the agency and then escorted me into the entrance and to the correct lift. The client very kindly drove me back to the airport during this journey I could see all the damage that had taken place during the war. The client explained to me how he escaped when Kuwait was invaded apparently having sent his family away he then drove for miles to get to the border.

On the day I visited the agency in Bahrain I again had a map and the route looked very straightforward. However, the driver took a road that did not follow the map and I queried it, his English was fair. We reached the town centre and then he still could not find the address. We stopped at a telephone box and he rang the agency, however, virtually all the staff were expats so I don't think the conversation was that easy. We drove to another street and I thought we were close so told him to stop and I got out. I went into a bathroom décor shop and asked if they knew the agency and fortunately it was in a building opposite. So I arrived for my appointment on time.

In order to help me deal with the travelling and working I made sure to take advantage of the massage facilities at the hotel to help relax the muscles.

It was very difficult to shake off this fatigue, ME call it what you will. After overseas trips I had to catch up on rest. Although I had regular GP appointments she told me that frankly there was nothing she could offer to improve the problem as there was no treatment, just a case of resting as much as possible. It was not very helpful especially when you work for yourself.

Business was still very slow and not helped by three publishers going into liquidation and consequently not paying our commission. Also one of the German publishers had decided not to renew our contract as we were now outside London. However, they owed us a considerable sum in commission. After trying the usual exchange of letters and faxes and statements requesting payment, finally I made the decision to instruct a lawyer. Unfortunately this lawyer seemed to be remarkably slow. It was a very protracted lawsuit but eventually the publisher's lawyer made an offer, however, our lawyers informed me that I could accept the offer or continue to a Court case, but if it went to Court the Judge would not be informed of the offer. Therefore, if we lost or at least were not necessarily awarded the same figure as the offer we may we worse off. After discussion with our Accountants I reluctantly decided to accept the offer.

I was still trying to find ways to exploit my late husband's music; I had a lot of money tied up in the recordings but of course it was difficult to promote as there was no-one to make any necessary changes. There was a music fair in New York and I booked to attend in the hope that I may make some contacts or have the opportunity to present some of the tapes. However, I did not find it that useful as it was mostly frequented by young musicians of various types. Again after attending some of the lectures and the exhibition area I needed to rest.

My health was still a concern, the GP seemed to be working on the basis that I was suffering from ME/Chronic Fatigue Syndrome caused by the last few years of excessive work-load combined with my late husband's illnesses and my mother's dementia followed by her death. Apart from excessive muscle aches and tiredness, she did not seem to consider any other possible reason. I noticed that I frequently had a bloated feeling and also that sometimes when I ate I got a pain down my back. The GP sent me for an X-ray on my spine and fortunately that was normal.

I remembered that many years ago, whilst on a press visit to the Balearic Islands I caught a stomach bug. This had returned intermittently and the hospital had told me that some virus infections can stay in the intestines and resurface whenever the person is tired or otherwise under the weather. To investigate the hospital had performed a barium enema X-ray, preceded by colonic irrigation. The X-ray had been normal. But afterwards I had not had any recurrence of the bug.

Therefore, I wondered if colonic irrigation may be helpful in this case. I spoke to the doctor about colonic irrigation and she found some names. She seemed to think I was slightly mad to wish to have the procedure but as I knew what it was like I wasn't so concerned. I contacted one of the therapists in Harley Street and made an appointment. After the first session, I immediately noticed that the bloated feeling had disappeared completely and also I no longer had the pain in my back when I ate.

The next few weeks I had several sessions with this therapist and started to feel some improvement. I hoped this would continue so that I could have the energy to work more normally without needing to keep resting. Mind you a lifetime of burning the candle at both ends probably had not helped.

CHAPTER TWENTY-EIGHT

Gradually we had to say goodbye to our three elderly cats, they were all around seventeen or eighteen but still it was sad to finally be without them; in particular Fred. Fred had really fought to carry on regardless of being a bit unstable on the hind legs and I think they had found the two kittens a little too much, especially Marilise who tried to flirt with Fluffy and practically pushed him over.

Before my husband had died he had wanted to buy me another cat, this time he wanted to get a Siamese cat. When my son heard this he started to look for kittens that may be available but I warned that it would not be any good as Michael would only get a cat if he was able to do it himself. In the event this did not happen and as we had now acquired two kittens I decided that I did not wish to add another.

However, I did want a dog and in 1995 started to look for available Golden Retriever puppies. I contacted one breeder but her dog's litter had now been purchased however she referred me to another breeder whose dog had just had a litter that would be available in a few weeks. I contacted this breeder and made an appointment to see the litter.

At this time my son was away on a TA camp and his girlfriend came with me to look at the puppies. They were adorable and the mother was with them and they were well looked after and living in the house. I saw a photograph of the sire. They were very dark gold and virtually all the puppies were matching colours. I had decided that I would like two puppies a male and female so I reserved two.

When my son came home we all went back to see the puppies and they were growing rapidly. They would be ready for collection in August. We all went to collect them. When we got home the two young cats Marilise and Maribel, who were about three-years old now, were inquisitive but when they saw the puppies they rushed upstairs and watched them from the landing with a certain amount of hissing through the bannisters. I named the puppies Paco and Bella.

We had to let the cats have their food on top of the chest freezer and fed them first to give the puppies the idea that the cats were in control.

We had discovered that both Marilise and Maribel had balance problems and their eyesight was not very good. Marilise was the only cat I had had which jumped onto a surface and tried to land with her back feet first teetering on the edge. Consequently we had made the decision that they must be house cats apart from trips into the garden which were supervised.

When the time came for Bella to go into season I had to put Paco into kennels as there was no way to ensure that they were separate and we did not want any accidents. Ultimately poor Paco was in kennels for a month and the kennel owner discouraged visits so as not to upset him. I was so pleased when I could go and collect him. He also seemed very pleased to see his sister. He was very fond of his sister and they enjoyed playing together.

Unfortunately, my health was not yet up to par and this was a lot of work so I had to enlist the help of my son and his girlfriend with the housetraining and starting the walking.

As my office was across the courtyard and I had part-time staff the puppies quickly got used to seeing other people and loved the attention.

Still trying to improve my fitness, I thought that perhaps I could re-visit flamenco dancing and found the details of a flamenco school which used a studio near Kings Cross, London. As I knew I would be many years older than the average student I talked to the owner and explained that I had learned to dance many years before and knew I would be out of practice but enquired whether it would be possible to join their beginners' class. She agreed that would not be a problem.

The classes were in the early evening and as I normally drove into London once a week I arranged to start the classes once a week because I was very out of practice. I had to get a new practice skirt and shoes. There was a dressmaker in Essex who specialized in flamenco dresses and I went to her for the skirt. Of course it was back to Anello and Davide well-known and long established makers of theatrical shoes. I continued the classes for some months

Early in 1996 the school announced they would have a Summer School in the August which would be held in Jerez, Spain. Now Jerez in August was going to be very hot but I loved Spain and after consideration I decided to book myself onto the course.

The school had booked the package, I checked out the hotel and found that it seemed to be quite good – at least it had room service. The information stated that the studio was air-conditioned so I thought that would make it much better to work in the heat that would be in Jerez at that time of year.

When I arrived at the hotel and settled in I found that

it was walking distance from the studio. After resting on the Sunday, Monday was time to start the course. It was arranged so that we had a morning of lessons and the rest of the day was free; although there were some social activities for anyone who wished.

The first morning I walked to the studio to find that it was actually in the basement and the closest thing to air-conditioning were two tiny fanlights at the top of the walls of the room which opened out at pavement level. That was it!

We changed into our practice skirts, tops etc. and then the lesson started. Flamenco lessons tend to be quite intense and these continued for about two hours. On the first morning I thought I was going to be sick or faint or both but dignity prevailed and I focused on the work and got through the first morning.

On leaving the studio to walk back to the hotel I reached the first café, sat down, ordered a Coca-Cola and tried to recover. Then carried on back to the hotel, took a shower and flaked out on the bed for the afternoon. Of course, I missed the socializing but it was the only way I could keep my strength up.

As the week went by I got through the lessons with less difficulty but still needed to rest. However, on several days by the end of the afternoon I took myself into the city of Jerez and looked around and, of course, went shopping.

I was pleased to get through the week and also on the Saturday each class put on a performance in the afternoon having also attended the class in the morning. I felt that in spite of the ME or whatever I had made progress and achieved something. Just to prove I had completed the course I received my Diploma.

I continued the classes back in London for several months but as it meant driving into London for them it was time consuming and I could not always go on the necessary day.

Although it was now a while since Michael had died I still found that at times I reacted if the phone rang early in the morning or late at night almost expecting to hear *'It's me'*. My reaction was the same if the doorbell rang at an unusual time – so many years of the erratic lifestyle I had lived with Michael never knowing when he would reappear. In some ways it helped because I imagine if you lose a partner when you have lived together day-in day-out you notice the emptiness more whereas I had spent most of my adult life running my life as well as a business. However, there had always been the anticipation of his return which, of course, was now impossible. When we married in 1990 I really thought that things had changed and I had hoped for a lengthy life together so in many ways I felt quite cheated. Although I am not entirely sure that I would have been suited to a conventional stay-at-home married life; that would probably have driven me to distraction. I needed to work but a reliable loving husband who did not wander would have been great.

CHAPTER TWENTY-NINE

I was contacted by someone who informed me that he was trying to open a small theatre in the West End. It was intended to be like the small workshop theatres which used to exist in the sixties; these allowed new shows and actors to present themselves to producers and agents. Harold informed me that he had formed a charity for this project and that he was getting most of the building materials and other help on a voluntary basis. He wanted some help with promotion to the press but only on an expenses basis. Above the building was a restaurant and he had made arrangements for catering for press attending the opening. I arranged a meeting when next in London. I thought the idea was good because most of the workshop theatres had been swallowed up with renovation and new building in the West End.

However, after all the invitations had been sent and replies received, I was suddenly informed that they would have to postpone the opening. Obviously if press have accepted a date it is difficult to get the same result with a change of date. I did not go into London for the first date but went for the new date. I discovered that some press had attended on the original date, so of course they were not going to come a second time. A day or so later

I was just leaving the house for the airport when Harold phoned and complained that he did not think there was sufficient press attendance. As I was not being paid for the service and they had made so many changes by this time my generosity was at an end. Some years later I found that actually the owner had turned the theatre into a complete commercial enterprise; so much for requesting services for charity.

By this time my son had moved out and was now living with his girlfriend in a house the other end of the town. He was doing a lot of camps and training so was away quite often. Although when he was home he came down to my office.

When Bella was spayed she went to stay with my son, the idea being that Paco would not be able to lick the wound or bother her. However, she managed to take the dressing apart herself and my son had to keep re-dressing it. After this I decided to let my son keep Bella. However, once she had recovered from the surgery he brought her to the house whenever he came down so the two dogs could continue to play together. Paco was obviously very fond of Bella.

I felt it was very lonely now living on my own – apart from the animals – Paco and the two cats. In fact it was the first time I had been completely on my own since I lived in my flat in Marylebone in the 1960s. However, it was good to have the work and most of the day was taken up with many business phone calls. I now had part-time secretarial help.

My girlfriend Rosemary suggested that a visit to a health spa might be a good idea. We settled on one and I drove there and Rosemary took the train and met me at the spa. When I went through the plan on arrival I stressed that I was not there to lose weight, just to relax. So I had the massages, facials and other relaxing treatments. It was a worthwhile trip and I was pleased that Rosemary had made the suggestion.

During the time that my husband and I had been at Midem one year we met a fellow from a German record label. At the time we were not able to do any business with them regarding Michael's works, however Hans contacted me and told me about a special line of CDs their company was producing and that they wanted to try to sell them in England. These were recordings of various classical works and the presentation was very expensive. The CDs were presented in special faux suede boxes with gold print, the German company regarded them as items that people would buy and display as well as play. Hans wanted my help to get some editorial and also to get into record companies and retail shops to sell them.

I took on the PR side and got editorial coverage with the well-known classical music magazines although if the review was critical the company did not appreciate it. We sold a few copies of the CDs for them. Finally there was a very special opera *"Etre Dieu"* **opéra-poème** apparently the work of Salvador Dali. I did a press release about this and was contacted by a freelance journalist who wished to write a story however we had to obtain various documents to prove that it was genuine Salvador Dali – there are many fake Dali works. Finally this was published as an extensive article in The Times. Subsequently, MTV contacted me as they wished to use the story and we sent them a copy of the Dali poster designed for the opera and it was broadcast on MTV.

Following that activity Dragan, the person who claimed to own the rights, contacted me directly to thank me for the editorial exposure. After that contact Dragan called a number of times and informed me that he was planning to mount a production of this opera and wanted to get a backer in the UK for the work. As only Dali could be it is a very strange production and the lyrics equally unusual.

I met with Dragan when he was in London and discussed the matter in detail and informed him that people would require absolute proof that he had the rights to the work and finally he supplied copies of various documents.

I contacted someone who had a client looking for somewhere to invest around one million pounds sterling and sent all the information. As is usual with these things the negotiations went on for a long time but finally they requested an actual financial breakdown of all the anticipated costs and eventually Dragan's accountant supplied this information. However, the proposed investor also wished to have details of the anticipated cast list for the production. Unfortunately, this is where it fell apart because it appeared that Dragan had not started to cast the production. He wanted to be sure he had the investment before approaching any actors or singers; further he did not seem to think he should have to supply this information, he considered the name Dali should be sufficient. In spite of many more calls and faxes the investor finally lost interest.

CHAPTER THIRTY

For many years we had specialized in representation of overseas travel and conference media and I had gathered much information on publications and exhibitions even those we did not represent. Frequently I gave assistance to clients with this information and in 1995 I decided that it would be possible to publish a directory. It was going to take a lot of work to research the information. I employed a couple of students during the summer and we sent out questionnaires to publishers, exhibition organizers, national tourist offices and other related companies to get the information.

It was decided that to create the directory we should use QuarkXPress program for setting and we bought the software and booked a training day for my son so that he could do the setting but also teach someone else to assist. We commissioned a local studio to create the artwork for the cover.

We were booked for a stand at World Travel Market in the autumn and we prepared flyers for advance promotion of the directory. The publications manager of WTO who was at a stand close by was interested and over the ensuing months we made an agreement that we would run a flash on the cover stating it was in association with WTO and they would buy 250 copies for distribution to their members. The first issue was in 1996 and went very well but was very costly to produce. So then we continued to update the information for the next edition. At this time everything was being done by fax and telephone more time consuming than it would have been if we had then had email.

By 1998 budgets were still slow and as I was on my own I had wondered about the possibility of selling the company but that type of business is not easy to sell. I did have one interested party but they were not interested in publishing the directory. We had some meetings but eventually they did not proceed to a sale. Therefore, I decided to continue on my own.

However, the funds I had invested in my late husband's music had resulted in taking an overdraft which of course was now having to be serviced without a great deal of chance of recouping from the music.

Although the house was not nearly as large as the London houses had been there were outbuildings used as the office and one that had been renovated for my husband's studio. The house had two acres of ground and stables in one of the paddocks. With a stream running through the garden and the main river at the end of the garden, it was very difficult to secure on my own.

Security was evidenced when one Sunday morning I was sitting at the breakfast table in the kitchen with the door open onto the patio and suddenly a group of teenagers started to cross the bridge that connected the patio to the garden. Annoyance overtook any concern about safety and I rushed outside and remonstrated with them. Finally I made them re-trace their footsteps all the way back to the river bank. On another occasion I was in the laundry room across the courtyard from the house and looked up to find two girls walking through the courtyard heading for the gate onto the road; obviously they had decided to take a short-cut. Again I rushed out and accosted them and made them walk back to the river. But this made me feel as though I needed to lock the front door when I was across the courtyard or in the garden.

I decided to do another down-size, so I put the house on the market. I found that the agents were not entirely sure how to value it with the land; they did not seem to be able to decide if the land and stables put much more value on the house. It took some time to sell. I was convinced that some viewers came just to see it without really intending to buy a house. After I had walked across the paddocks and shown the whole property to one couple I asked about their own sale only to find that they were just gathering information for friends returning from Hong Kong in the near future. I was furious with the agents because they should have been more selective about appointments to view.

Whilst my son was still living at the house, one Saturday morning I was still resting in bed and there was an enormous crash and I discovered that a car had hit the outer wall of the house and then bounced off and come to a halt against the forge. It was a shock and caused cracks to the outer wall. So when I came to sell because of its position I knew that someone may ask questions about traffic. One viewer whom the agents had informed me was a lawyer, I expected detailed questions and sure enough she asked if there had ever been any traffic problems, so I had to declare that a car had hit the house. I really didn't see much point in continuing with the viewing.

While the house was on the market I had started to house-hunt and found another smaller period house in the same town unfortunately the garden was very small but it was only a few minutes' walk from an excellent dog walking area. Unfortunately, after a few weeks I lost the house because the vendors had already moved and they received another offer with a buyer ready to proceed. I viewed several other houses nearby but either the vendors took the property off the market or in one instance the vendor accepted my offer and went on holiday. When I next heard from the agents the vendor had returned from holiday and increased the price by £10,000 so I withdrew the offer.

Finally my agents found a buyer but it dragged on with the agent stating the buyer did not require a mortgage but no indication of a survey being booked. I had contacted removal companies and because of all the office documents and equipment as well as the studio equipment, I knew that some items would have to go into store. The removal company said it would be a three-day move. Eventually I received a call to say that the buyer wished to exchange contracts and then complete four days later. Which was ridiculous timing; there was no way I could arrange that in the four days. The agents suggested another removal company I contacted them and when they came to quote agreed it was a 3-day move. But as the move was at such short notice temporarily everything would have to be in store with the removal company.

At the time I was selling The Forge I saw an ad for houses in Mazarrón in Spain. I remembered Mazarrón from a holiday when we were driving through and at that time it was a very unspoiled place with a beautiful beach. The prices were very low and I decided to go on an inspection visit; it occurred to me that when I found a new house in England it might be useful to let that and live in Spain – something I had considered on and off for many years.

The inspection flight was a very early morning flight. My son was away and I had to drive to Gatwick. His girlfriend looked after the dogs and cats. I left really early in the morning and managed to get to Gatwick without losing myself! We flew to Murcia airport (San Javier) and were met by a representative. I stayed at an aparthotel owned by the developer but the heating was non-existent. However, next morning we were driven to the development. I looked at the bungalows and following the full inspection decided to buy off-plan. The development was about ten minutes' drive from Mazarrón. I was delighted to find that the beach at Mazarrón was still unspoilt. The property was due to be completed early in 1999.

By this time my son was not working with me and I was trying to persuade him that making a start on packing his belongings would be helpful as it would have to be done before I moved.

One day my son came in with details of a house in a nearby market town. It was a Grade II listed property, in fact a renovation of two houses into one. The photos showed that it had masses of exposed timbers and of course there was no chain. I went to view the house a couple of times and requested a few alterations and as my sale was now closing I decided to purchase this property. However, in spite of no upward chain the fact that my sale was suddenly completing so quickly it meant that I would not have the usual few weeks for the exchange of contract and completion of my purchase. The lawyers for my purchase would not proceed without all the necessary searches and even with the best will in the world this takes time.

Moving house is always tiring and stressful and this move was no different. The day before the move my son's friend came to help and at one point I asked him to get something from the barn; as there were stables and barns he came back to ask which one and I told him the one with the lawnmower – it was a ride-on mower. He returned again to tell me that there was no mower. He was an intelligent young man and obviously would recognize a mower however I went down to the paddock with him and to my horror discovered that the mower had gone. The paddock gate had been chained and padlocked and the chain was cut, this gate led onto the river pathway where the water company had a gate over the weir and that had been taken off its hinges. These are expensive and would be conspicuous if driven down the road so whoever stole it must have used a trailer but, of course, it was too far from the house for it to have been heard in the house. The fact that it had been kept safely in the barn for several years I came to the conclusion that it must have been stolen by someone who knew when the move was to take place. I had to contact the police and the insurance company.

I had to put my furniture in store for a few weeks and stay at my son's house - which was not the most comfortable of options. There was one small spare bedroom but I had my computer in there as well as both cats. Paco was able to be with his sister in the house. I took an office facility a few miles away for calls to be referred and post to be delivered and then had to try and work from the house.

Finally the completion of my purchase was going to be able to take place just a few days before Christmas and I moved into the new house. It started snowing on the day while I was standing outside instructing the removal men which items were to go into the storage container that I had arranged and which were coming into the house.

Critically just as this was taking place my son had informed me that his girlfriend had broken off the engagement and gone home to her mother's for Christmas and he was moving into the new house with me. He was understandably very upset about his situation and although he was now supposed to be helping me with settling everything to get unpacked he was so preoccupied with the breakup that he was not concentrating at all.

Both the dogs and cats were now being settled into

the new house. The garden was a relatively small walled garden and when the dogs went into it they ran to the bottom and both stopped and looked around, if they could have spoken I think it would have been *'is this it?'* They looked so surprised – The Forge had two acres.

In the midst of this upheaval we celebrated Christmas and a friend of my son came over as he was working at a radio station nearby.

Paco with sister Bella

CHAPTER THIRTY-ONE

By mid-January I had to go to Madrid for a trade fair and as I had been informed that the bungalow in Spain was completed I arranged to go down to Mazarrón to see the property and accept the keys and then up to Madrid for the Fair. When I saw the bungalow I was very surprised to see that although a bungalow there was a steep flight of steps up to the front door. At first I thought it was the wrong house, but was assured it was not. All the properties I had seen on the inspection visit had been on the flat but as the land was undulating they had built bungalows on the various levels thus mine was one with this flight of stairs.

However, the deeds were not ready on that occasion so I had to go back to Spain a few weeks later to visit the Notary to deal with the deeds and other paperwork. On this occasion I visited the house and arranged for the furniture, including bedding, white goods and all the other basic necessities for living and letting.

I planned to use the property for vacations but also for holiday rentals. I found a lady who also lived on the urbanization who was prepared to clean the bungalow and deal with laundry for change-over for holiday rentals.

We were in the process of producing the next edition of the directory – Travel Media Directory – and at that time my son was helping with setting the directory. However, he was away at training camps and still dealing with the break-up of his engagement as well as looking for another job instead of working with my business. So one way and another he was quite distracted. We were working long hours to get the directory ready for print.

In addition I had to travel to other trade fairs so then my son was looking after the dogs and cats as well as the other work. Finally we had the directory set and ready to go to the printers.

My son had an interview at a major publishing company and following some subsequent interviews was offered a position of electronic marketing manager for one of the divisions.

Soon after he started his new job his ex-fiancé made contact with him and I discovered they started to meet again. Not long after he moved back in with her.

So a few months after arriving at my new house I was now living alone again apart, of course, for my dog Paco and the cats Marilise and Maribel. Paco definitely missed his sister Bella he had obviously enjoyed it whilst she was at the house as they played together.

As I was now working alone I had to use an answering machine for calls whilst I was out or away as so far email was not automatically used by all clients and certainly not by many of the overseas publishers.

My son was now immersed in his new job and working long hours so could be difficult to contact or see.

I still travelled to other trade fairs be it London, Madrid, Berlin or Milan. World Travel Market had started to offer publishers space on a stand on the basis of 'media partners' in return for advertising, so obviously publishers were not any longer prepared to pay to participate on our stand so we had to stop taking our own stand. There was an advantage insofar as we no longer had to staff the stand or for that matter ship large quantities of magazines and clear up afterwards. Also I could reduce the number of days at the Fair.

Not long after the purchase of my house in Spain I unexpectedly ran into Molly a girlfriend of many years although we had not seen each other for a few years. Molly came to stay for the weekend and we discussed the house in Spain. She was very interested and decided she might like to investigate buying in Spain as well. Shortly afterwards she called me to say she had visited Catalonia and bought a town house. Apparently it required a lot of work and she went back and forth whilst having the work done. I am not sure that her son was equally enthusiastic but then he did not always regard his mother's decisions as well founded.

After that Molly and I kept in touch and she spent quite a lot of time in Spain although keeping her apartment near London. Molly was an artist; in the village where her house was located she could sit out in the square with her easel and paint which also helped her to meet local people. We often Skyped and she would show me her latest paintings. Quite soon she bought a second house and subsequently she sold the first one. The problem with the town houses though is that the old ones do not use the ground floor for living so it is necessary to use the stairs for the living rooms and then another floor for the bedrooms. As Molly had a heart condition she started to find the stairs a problem and then bought a bungalow just outside the village. Finally she decided to sell her apartment back in England and buy a new apartment in Spain. She told me that this was much easier, everything on one floor, lift, car parking and, even better neighbours she could turn to if she was unwell. She tried to sell the bungalow but found that very difficult so let it as much as she could. As she was living in Catalonia she found that locally it was necessary to try to use Catalan instead of Spanish and that was more difficult but she was trying hard to learn Catalan.

CHAPTER THIRTY-TWO

Just after my son had settled into his new company he invited me to lunch at Easter and he and his girlfriend announced that they had decided to marry at the end of May. That meant there was not a great deal of time and as I very often made my own dresses I decided I had better get a move on and start sewing. They were marrying down in the West Country where they had friends who could provide a choir. I made a dress and jacket in burnt orange silk and selected an appropriate wedding hat.

Unfortunately they had chosen a Bank Holiday weekend and I had to drive down which ended up by taking seven hours. By the time I arrived at the hotel I was exhausted and then discovered there was a dinner for family and close friends that evening.

As I would be on my own I had asked my son if he would invite my friend Rosemary and her husband to the wedding so I had close friends with me. The Chapel used for the wedding was delightful and the wedding went off well. After the reception they departed for the honeymoon and that evening I had dinner with my girlfriend. The next morning I drove back to London. I stayed in London because the following day I was travelling to Geneva for a trade fair. Yet another example of pushing myself too far because I only attended the fair for one day, flew back, stayed in London another night and then drove back to

Suffolk. Of course, once home I had to go and collect Paco from kennels and the cats from the cattery.

The next month I went down to the house in Spain theoretically for a rest. I arrived late in the evening but whilst unpacking decided to put some things into the washing machine. I was in the bedroom unpacking and putting clothes away when I looked out onto the hallway to see a sea of bubbles. I discovered these were emanating from the washing machine. At home in England I normally had plenty of newspapers around which are good for mopping up but I only had a couple and I spread these out to try to stop the water going into the bedroom. I had switched off the washing machine but had no idea why it was flooding bubbles. Over the next days I ran the machine several times empty and without any powder and eventually the bubbles stopped. Apart from anything else, I needed everything to be working because the following week I had holiday guests renting the bungalow. When I finally reached the cleaner she admitted that she had subcontracted the work and the woman who had last used the machine had put washing-up liquid into it instead of washing powder. It was just fortunate that it happened when I was at the house and not a holiday guest.

A month or so later one day I did not feel very well, it was difficult to put my finger on it but I had slight pains in my arms. I took the dog out but mostly sat by the river and then came back. I did not fancy much food and eventually by early evening phoned the doctor but by then I was referred to the out-of-hours service. When I spoke to a doctor I explained the symptoms and was asked to go to the surgery. I drove myself there and the doctor examined me. My blood pressure was up, although I had had high blood pressure for years it had always been controlled; I explained this was not normal. The doctor did not seem to be able to decide what to do and finally sent me home but told me to call my own doctor next morning. When I got home I called my son to let him know I was unwell. I did not sleep during the night but felt really awful.

The out-of-hours doctor phoned early the next morning, I am sure just to check I was still alive on his watch. I phoned my doctor's surgery to request a home visit. During the morning a GP arrived, took my blood pressure and again did not seem to take much notice of it being high because I have high blood pressure and I explained that this was unusually high. I requested an ECG and really had to fight to get this and even when she agreed she said I would not want it for a while, so it was over a week before I got the ECG. My daughter-in-law arrived whilst this discussion ensued. I went back to bed. My son came to see me in the evening and I was still feeling unwell. I stayed in bed most of the week. Eventually I had the ECG and as soon as it was complete the nurse asked me to wait and then came back with a glass of water and aspirin for me to drink and an appointment to see my GP later that afternoon. I knew that obviously there was something wrong. When I saw the GP he told me that unfortunately I had suffered a heart attack and I would be referred to the cardiologist. He ensured that they had all my contact details indicating that I should expect an appointment quickly as this was an urgent appointment.

A couple of weeks went by and no appointment so I called the GP who did not seem surprised and gave me the telephone number for the consultant's secretary. When I spoke with her she indicated the appointment would be about five months hence. This seemed a long time for an 'urgent' appointment. Finally I checked to see if I could get a private appointment and subsequently saw the consultant within a couple of weeks. When I discussed this with the consultant he told me that the GP's office must have used the wrong fax number as there was a dedicated number for urgent appointments and the hospital would have had to see me within a couple of weeks.

At this consultation the doctor informed me that I must now avoid all red meat – beef, lamb, pork, bacon and also reduce dairy such as butter, cream, cheese. I realized it was goodbye to steak au poivre, steak and kidney pie, rare roast beef. Although I already ate chicken I realized that several of the dishes I prepared which had cream or crème fresh sauces were added to the exclusion list. Toasted sandwiches with bacon or cheese were also now off the menu. Down to skimmed milk. No ice cream. Actually the list of exclusions seemed endless the more I thought about it.

The consultant arranged for an exercise stress test and when I took this he was in the room as well as the technician. I thought I was going to expire but he encouraged me to keep going and I reached the target he was expecting. As I always wore heels at the last minute I had to grab a pair of flat shoes.

Following the appointment he said that this test should be repeated at the end of the year which was three months or so away. Additional medication was prescribed. I made every effort to cut out all the food that had been put on the no-go list. Previously I had not been a particular fan of fish but decided I had better try to make myself like it or least eat it.

Whilst I had not been hospitalized it took a while for me to start to feel more energetic but for the same reason nobody seemed to take the matter very seriously. As I was now working on my own obviously I had to continue to undertake whatever work came in. This event just proved something I had read regarding heart attacks in women – they do not necessarily present in the same way as in men and can easily be missed.

With my friend Rosemary at my son's wedding 2001

CHAPTER THIRTY-THREE

By the time we reached mid-December I was looking after my son's dog who was my dog's sister and on a fairly wintery day decided to put them in the car and drive them a few miles to give them an off-lead walk. I got part way through the walk, part of which was uphill and decided it was time to stop. I turned around and called the dogs back. The ground was extremely muddy and I heard my dog running and knew it took him some distance to stop; I tried to move to the side – too late within seconds I was up in the air and sat down on the ground with sharp pain in the left leg. I looked down and my foot was definitely facing in the wrong direction. I thought I must have broken my ankle. I was sitting in the mud with two golden retrievers running around and coming back to me as though they wondered why I was sitting on the ground. I had their leads round my neck and these had disappeared in the fall. Although the area is a popular dog-walking route so far that morning I had not encountered any other walkers. I reached for my phone to call the paramedics and suddenly realized that I was on a muddy pathway under trees alongside a field and wondered where the 999 call centre was located and if they would know where I was located. I decided to call my son first to tell him where I was so that at least he could check that I had been found. By sheer coincidence he was driving towards the town and he called emergency.

I was quite a way from the parking area, and shortly a paramedic trudged up to me, panting and commenting it was a long way. As I was recovering from a heart attack I wondered how he was going to get me back to an ambulance. He started to look at my leg and then my son arrived. The paramedic decided it would be too difficult to use the ambulance so he called in a helicopter. It arrived shortly and as I was loaded onto it my son's parting words instructed me not to be sick because it costs a bomb to clean them. When I reached the hospital I was X-rayed and, in fact, I had broken the tibia and fibular. It was set and eventually I was taken to a ward. Fortunately, my son had taken charge of the dogs and would have arranged for my car to be moved.

Once in the ward with my leg in plaster from thigh to foot I was suitably immobile. I had explained about the heart attack a few months earlier and they had left the plaster open to allow for any swelling but also with the possibility that it would set without surgery. It was not particularly painful until the physio people turned up one day. They started to prod it around and from then onwards it was more uncomfortable. I was taken back to X-ray and it was not set right so I had to have it reset which meant back to theatre. A doctor came to see me and ordered some cardiac tests. Unfortunately as I had seen the cardiac consultant privately it seemed that no records had been transferred back to the NHS system so the doctor did not have any of the records. Some hours after I had the tests the doctor could not find the results; he even asked me if I had definitely had the tests. Eventually they decided to take me to theatre. Somewhat disconcerting, the anaesthetist made a mess of inserting the needle and passed my hand to an assistant as though it was a spare part; he then proceeded to investigate the other hand. Obviously he succeeded because I next remember the recovery room and eventually back to the ward.

Christmas was approaching and an occupational therapist came to visit me and went through all the questions. My house was a timber framed 600 year old property so there were various small steps between rooms and a narrow winding staircase up to my bedroom. However, apparently I did not qualify for any carers. My son phoned a raft of care agencies but none had any carers available. The hospital decided to send me home on Christmas Eve and my son and daughter-in-law brought my cats back and the dogs. Immediately after Boxing Day they tried some more agencies and finally one agency had a carer available. She was prepared to feed the cats as well so they could stay with me. My son was due to go away with a group of friends for New Year so the dogs had to go into kennels. When my son came back my dog had to stay at his house so I did not see him for quite a while.

A single bed had been placed downstairs and screened off from the dining room. When the carer came in the mornings she helped me into the sitting room and I was surrounded by the phone and laptop with snacks on the table. She came in morning, lunch time and early evening. Fortunately she was prepared to help me into my office so that I could print out anything required and take items to the post office.

Fortunately during this time I was very busy with work so although I was more or less restricted to the house I did not have much time to get bored as I could concentrate on work. However, the downside of the carer's visit was that the evening visit was around 6.0pm. which meant that she had to ensure I was then in bed. The cats were very pleased as they chose to come and sleep on my bed.

As time went by the plaster was reduced to below the knee and later to one that I could remove in order to wash. By this time I could get myself upstairs for bed which allowed me to be able to actually go to bed at a more sensible time. After six months finally the plaster was removed. I asked the Consultant when I could go back to heels – she advised to wait a while. But she said that I could start to drive again. I got the carer to come with me whilst I drove the car around the block it was very painful pressing down on the clutch. My dog came back but it was very painful to walk him for a while because of course my foot had been immobile and I was not given any physiotherapy.

Just before I had the accident I had cut out the material to make a coat and once the plaster on my leg was reduced so that I was more mobile I asked the carer to bring my sewing machine downstairs and I spent weekends making the coat so that I finished it by the time I was out of plaster.

Apart from walking shoes I wore with the dog, all my shoes were high heels. I kept trying on my shoes to see which I could walk in but at first none were possible. I went to the nearest shoe shop which fortunately stocked shoes from several continental manufacturers. Finally I bought several pairs of low heeled shoes from a Spanish supplier and had to wear these. I still wanted to get back to my heels but after several weeks I came to the realization that I was going to have to give up some of the highest heels. I very begrudgingly put aside several pairs of shoes which I would have to take to the charity shop.

During the time my leg had been healing my son had been given an injection into his back as the hospital hoped this would improve the problems he had experienced for some time with back pain. The problems had originated during his parachute course some years before because although he did not appear to have had an accident apparently on the descent he was blown against the side of a barn.

However, after a while the surgeon decided that the injection was not going to be the answer and discussed the possibility of surgery. Surgery on the spine is not to be decided lightly and my son had to look into all the aspects of the procedure and discuss this with his wife. Finally he decided to accept the surgical route. The hope was that although it might not cure the problem it should give him a good improvement and reduction in pain. It is a long and serious surgery so I visited before he went to theatre and then once he was back in his room. It was going to take an extended period for recovery.

Maureen Wingham photo-shoot 2002

CHAPTER THIRTY-FOUR

The next time I went down to my house in Spain I found it very difficult to carry my luggage up the steep stairs to the house. Obviously following the somewhat badly handled heart attack these steep stairs were going to be a problem. Eventually I had to unpack my case in the car and take clothes upstairs a few at the time.

I knew that the developers were going to build a second phase of the urbanization and some of the properties were slightly larger but still bungalows. I started to consider the possibility of selling my present bungalow because I couldn't continue to have the difficulty getting luggage in and out of the house as well as shopping it hardly made for a relaxing holiday retreat.

When I made my next visit to Mazarrón I selected an estate agent and made the preparations to sell the bungalow. I was fortunate that the agents got a sale within three months and I went back to Spain to deal with all the legal matters and last but not least to get the payment.

Before I returned to England I investigated the properties being built in the next phase of the urbanization and was shown the bungalows; these were slightly larger and they had a much larger roof terrace with the staircase to it built as part of the original plan. I selected a house off-plan and the agents said that the completion should be about one year. I signed the contract and paid the deposit.

This time I was considering that I might move down and live there when the house was complete or alternatively perhaps spend the winters down there.

After Michael passed away I continued to send his mother cards for Birthday, Mother's Day and Christmas so when I was informed that she had passed away when Mother's Day came it seemed very strange not to have anyone to send a card as my own mother had passed away several years before.

Although the house I had bought about four years ago had stunning beams and exposed timbers and was Grade II listed it was difficult to heat to keep me warm. It was not easy to exclude all the drafts and I think the builder who renovated the property had been economical with the central heating. I decided to have the property valued and put it up for sale.

This was not as easy as I had hoped; I changed agents several times then the agent informed me we had a sale. I put an offer on another property and then it all fell apart, the potential buyers did not get their finance. The house went back on the market and this time I told the agents I did not want a sale board up until the actual sale had gone through. Naturally I in turn had to pull out of the property on which I had put an offer. There was little point in looking at more properties until another sale was on the horizon.

Towards the end of 2004 my girlfriend Rosemary phoned to tell me that her husband had passed away. Although they had married in 1992 their relationship had spanned many years before it was finally possible for them to marry. Although she had been fortunate to have more years of marriage than I had, her husband's death occurred within a few weeks after her mother passed away. Understandably she was very distressed. Something we had in common.

Rosemary had moved to Gloucestershire when she married so she was on the other side of the country which meant to meet up it was only convenient when we both went into London. We had known each other since our teens so we had a lot of history and I enjoyed the occasional lunches and telephone conversations.

Whereas Spain had always been the country I was most likely to visit – or consider living – Rosemary had a particular affinity with Italy. Following her husband's demise she often talked about the idea of moving to Italy, although on one occasion when she rented an apartment in Rome she found the long flight of stairs difficult with luggage in the same way that I had with my bungalow in Spain. A sign that we were, of course, both getting older.

The new house in Spain was progressing more slowly than planned in fact it was way over schedule although the agents sent computer updates.

I returned from an overseas trip and noticed that my cat Marilise seemed to have a slight swelling at the side of her nose. I took her to the Vet and they kept her in for surgery. They had to remove a tooth in order to access the tumour. However, the Vet thought that she should be referred to a specialist Vet near Cambridge. We took her to Dick White Referrals and the Vet said he would operate to endeavour to get the whole of the tumour. After a few days we were able to collect her. She looked good, he had obviously made a very neat job but he was concerned that he could not get sufficient margin around the tumour that he would normally hope to achieve for complete success. We took her home.

During her visits and absences from home Paco had not seemed to be too concerned and neither had Marilise's sister. However, once Marilise was home she had frequent appointments for check-ups and then the tumour had obviously returned. There came the time when it was decided that I must say goodbye to Marilise and on that occasion the Vet euthanized her. When I returned home I left the carrier in the garage so as not to take it into the house empty. However, as soon as I got into the house Paco was immediately anxious; he went into the garden and ran around. Although on other occasions I had returned without her he obviously knew this was different.

A few weeks later my son phoned me to tell me that their dog Bella was ill and the Vet had kept her in for tests. It appeared to be serious. The next day he phoned again to say that the Vet had referred Bella to a specialist some miles away and they were taking her there. They were planning to visit her the following morning and I arranged to go with them. However, late that evening he called me again as he had received a phone call to say she had already deteriorated so they were going early the next morning. I called my neighbour and asked if they would come in a couple of times to let Paco into the garden whilst I was out.

Unfortunately, when we arrived at the clinic the next day it was very obvious that Bella was very ill. The consultant was suggesting that they may be able to give her chemotherapy but even it if worked the most it would give her would be about six months. She was vomiting blood. As sad as it would be I thought that it was probably more humane to euthanize now rather than put her through some stressful treatment with the possibility of limited success. However, as she was now my son's dog it had to be their decision. Finally that decision was made and we were all with her at the end.

When I got back home my neighbour phoned me to find out what had happened. I told her the news and she said that they were surprised at Paco's behaviour. He was always keen to play ball but she said that the second time they went into the house for once he was very quiet and did not want to play.

I had to take Paco to the Vet; because he had a gluten allergy he was prone to digestive upsets but it took some weeks to get him settled and the Vet thought that losing Marislie and his sister within about six weeks had upset him.

I had been concerned that Maribel may be lonely without her sister however she obviously was not missing Marilise. Marilise had been a bit mean to Maribel often hissing at her and even swiping her with her paw. Now Maribel was very confident and strutting about the house even taking into account that she had bad eyesight and balance problems. She got very close to Paco and the two were really good friends over the next few years.

I was still trying to sell my home and still changed agents but finally the original agent sent a potential buyer just before Christmas. The husband came alone and told me at present they were living in one of the small villages and he thought that the town would be more convenient. After Christmas he visited again with his wife. Then there was the usual wait and chase with the agents. At last there was a firm offer which I accepted but of course now I had to house hunt. I looked at a property in a village but decided that as I had never lived in a village with or without shops now was not the time of life to start village life. I needed to be somewhere where there was easy access to doctors, Vets, rail station and shops. Although I had intended to move a little further away I finally settled on a house further down the same road. It was a period property but with a much larger garden so that would be better for the dog. It was not listed thus it had the benefit of double glazing which would make it easier to keep warm also the staircase had been replaced with a modern style which was much easier. Eventually the sale went through and the completion date was set for the end of

April almost exactly seventeen years after we first moved to Suffolk.

When I moved into the house it was necessary to replace all the central heating and upgrade the electrics as well as replace the flooring in the reception room and have the floors upstairs stripped. It was very fortunate that it was very good weather whilst the work was being done so although builders tend to have windows and doors open I did not freeze. After a few months the work including the decorating had been completed. I was still working and had to use the single bedroom as a study.

By the October I was informed that the new house in Spain was complete so I made arrangements to go down to inspect it. I stayed at the hotel in Puerto de Mazarrón and drove to the urbanization. I called at the developer's office and collected the keys and got the directions to the house. As I drove down one road I noticed that the same style property as mine had steep flights of steps and thought that history was repeating itself. However, the land was undulating and when I reached my property it was with relief to find only a couple of steps up to the front terrace. The salon also had a dining area and led onto the rear patio. There was a flight of steps up to the roof terrace which was much larger than at the previous house.

I returned to the developer's office and paid the cheque for the final tranche and signed the receipt for the keys. This house had come with a basic furniture package, so I did not have to get tables, beds, sofas and so forth. However, I did have to get the necessary white goods.

As I wanted to try to let as soon as possible I started to get cutlery and linen and kitchen ware. I also needed linen for all the beds and towels. I was put in touch with a lady who ran a cleaning service particularly for holiday rentals. She also had several expat contacts that lived locally for various handyman jobs.

I was informed that the deeds were not yet available but when I bought the previous house they were not available for a few weeks so I was not particularly concerned. By now the house was completely furnished. Although the furniture package had included some light fittings I had changed most of these and included ceiling fans.

Although in my previous house I had not had a television, I realized that by this time the English visitors seemed to regard television as a necessity so I had a dish fitted on the roof but only bought a small television set. Also I had an awning fitted on the rear patio.

I met some residents and learned that none of them had yet signed their deeds. I spoke with the estate agents and was informed that the deeds should be available very soon. Most of these agents were expats.

I visited a few more times but still the deeds were not available. Also I enquired about the Certificate of First Habitation because that is necessary for services such as electricity, water and telephone to be connected; until it is available the properties are supplied by the builders supply. Every time I made enquiries about this Certificate I was advised that it was the local Council which was very slow and delayed everything.

When I returned to England I undertook some further research regarding the necessary Certificate of First Habitation and the deeds. I spoke to someone who undertook surveys for clients and he informed me that on an urbanization a little further up the coast, owners had been waiting for fourteen years and still did not have the Certificate. He advised me to try to cancel the contract because by this time the utility companies were much stricter about connecting the services. Also until the Certificate was available it would be difficult to sell the property.

Finally I reached the developer's lawyer who admitted

that so far they had not applied for the Certificate because they had not yet completed the necessary infrastructure so it could be a year or more. This set alarm bells ringing.

Further research connected me to a firm of lawyers which appeared to be concentrating on offering their services to expat purchasers. I sent them copies of the Contract and other documentation and following telephone calls and email exchanges they advised me that I had grounds to seek a legal cancellation of the Contract. Although I liked the house and would have liked to have stayed there I discovered that the services supplied by the developers were beginning to be disrupted and realized that this would be a problem if I was letting to holiday makers. One resident informed me that the site manager was knocking on doors demanding €100 for the electricity supplies. Reluctantly I decided to instruct the lawyers to start the legal proceedings.

There was the possibility of two reasons for cancellation, first being the lack of the Certificate of First Habitation and the second was the fact that the poligono on which my house was located had been designated as only touristic which in theory meant that it could not actually be used as a residential home. The Contract had not made any reference to the properties on this poligono being for touristic purposes. As far as I was concerned I considered that the lawyers should go for both reasons to cancel the contract. I was assured that they would take both into consideration when drafting the lawsuit. However, this would be after months of exchanges of many emails.

Little did I realize that apart from my usual work I was about to embark on a long and time consuming legal wrangle over what should have been my prospective retirement home. Obviously I was not going to be moving to Spain or, in fact, letting the house. But that's another saga.

View to Golf Course at Camposol, Mazarrón - Spain

Pto. Mazarrón with view of beach - Spain

Pto. Mazarron – Spain

www.ingramcontent.com/pod-product-compliance
Lightning Source LLC
Chambersburg PA
CBHW051943290426
44110CB00015B/2086